The Foundations of Threat Hunting

Organize and design effective cyber threat hunts to meet business needs

Chad Maurice

Jeremy Thompson

William Copeland

BIRMINGHAM—MUMBAI

The Foundations of Threat Hunting

Copyright © 2022 Packt Publishing

Group Product Manager: Vijin Boricha

Publishing Product Manager: Shrilekha Malpani

Senior Editor: Arun Nadar

Content Development Editor: Sujata Tripathi

Technical Editor: Shruthi Shetty

Copy Editor: Safis Editing

Project Coordinator: Shagun Saini

Proofreader: Safis Editing

Indexer: Tejal Daruwale Soni

Production Designer: Vijay Kamble

Marketing Coordinator: Hemangi Lotlikar

First published: June 2022

Production reference: 1130522

Published by Packt Publishing Ltd.
Livery Place
35 Livery Street
Birmingham
B3 2PB, UK.

ISBN 978-1-80324-299-6

www.packt.com

To my wife and children, thank you for all of the love and support over the years. You give everything meaning and have made this journey possible.

– Chad Maurice

To my wife and family, thanks for the love and patience over the years and the extra support during the writing of this book. For all the Airmen I served with, thanks for helping me get to where I am today – aim high!

– Jeremy Thompson

For my wife and friends, who have continued to support me through all of life's ups and downs.

– William Copeland

Foreword

I have known William Copeland, Chad Maurice, and Jeremy Thompson for a combined 20 years. Each one of them is an information security professional who has continued to push evolution onto the organizations they have been a part of. They are not only technically proficient analysts but also knowledgeable leaders who understand how to balance an organization's operational requirements with their security needs in order to minimize exposure to emerging threats while maximizing effectiveness in the business landscape. Each one of these authors has led security teams in the pursuit of securing and hunting across multimillion-dollar networks while continuing to evolve their strategies to defend these networks from some of the most advanced malicious actors in the world.

Over the last 10 years, there has been a growing shift in **Security Operations Centers (SOCs)** to move beyond their past mindsets. These SOCs were initially built to simply respond to alerts and potentially "*find bad*" while it was happening or had already happened on a network. This reactive approach leaves a company and its network catching the problem too late and thereby just finding the data breach and subsequent exfiltration of data months to years after it has already left the network. For this reason, SOCs have taken a more proactive approach, hiring penetration testers to find holes in their network defense before a malicious actor does, while also performing threat hunts to find out where those same actors have already slipped past defenses.

You may be wondering, what is a hunt? How does a team perform this task? Where is a good place to start? If you asked any of these questions, or maybe you are just looking for a different perspective on how to conduct a hunt on your network, *The Foundations of Threat Hunting* is for you. This book helps you to understand how to put a team together, how to plan a hunt (a very crucial step), and how to use the data your SOC is collecting in order to assist the hunt.

Additionally, this book will help you understand threat intelligence and how to use it to improve your hunt. As a person who has performed several hunts, I cannot overstate the assistance that finding and utilizing threat intelligence properly can be to your hunt.

In *The Foundations of Threat Hunting*, you are being given over 30 years of combined knowledge and perspective on threat hunting and cybersecurity. This information is provided to you in an understandable and relatable way. Using instruction and stories to help bridge knowledge and application, you will understand threat hunting and be able to execute an effective hunt on your network.

Evolve your SOC into a proactive phase and begin threat hunting with *The Foundations of Threat Hunting*.

Anthony Particini

Threat Hunt Lead and Instructor (GCIH, GCFA)

Contributors

About the authors

Chad Maurice is a life-long cybersecurity enthusiast with a background in both offensive and defensive teams. He has led Red Teams in physical and network security assessments as well as overseen planning and daily management for numerous incident response and threat hunting teams that provided defenses for enterprise networks spanning the globe.

He earned a master's degree in information systems security/information assurance from Capella University in 2011. Additionally, Chad has achieved an array of industry certifications ranging from OSCP to CISSP. Currently, he is an engineer at a Fortune 100 company, enhancing defensive capabilities for all of their business assets.

Jeremy Thompson is a tenacious leader and technical expert who has dedicated the last two decades of his life to the profession of cybersecurity. His background includes broad experience from managing infrastructure in support of a large-scale network to directing operations for an organization conducting threat hunts on IT and OT networks around the globe.

He earned a master's degree in information systems management from the University of Nebraska at Omaha in 2014. Additionally, Jeremy has achieved the following certifications: CCNA – Cyber Operations, GSEC, GCFA, GDAT, GFNA, and CISSP. Currently, he is an incident response and operations manager for CyberDefenses Inc out of Austin, TX.

William Copeland is a renowned leader and technician within the cyber defense community. He has endeavored, over the last two decades, to clear the path for the operators under his leadership to become more efficient and effective cyber defenders.

He earned a bachelor's degree in information technology from Western Governors University in 2018. Additionally, William has the following certifications: Security+, Linux+, Project+, Network+, GCFA, GPEN, GNFA, GREM, GDAT, GCDA, GSEC, GCIA, GCIH, SSAP, GCFE, and GCTI. Currently, he is a senior leader within a cyber hunting organization, providing planning, coordination, integration, and execution of defensive teams that track and eradicate adversaries on customer networks.

About the reviewer

Mostafa Yahia is a senior threat hunter and DFIR analyst with over 6 years of experience in hunting, detection, and response to cyber threats. Currently, he works at one of the largest cybersecurity companies in Egypt. He holds a bachelor's degree in computer science and has achieved extensive training and certifications through SANS, IBM, FireEye, and Cisco.

I'd like to thank my wife, Menna, for her love and support. I'd also like to thank our son, Omar, for giving me positive energy and always making me smile.

Table of Contents

3

Team Construct

4

Communication Breakdown

5

Methodologies

6

Threat Intelligence

7

Planning

Part 2: Execution – Conducting a Hunt

8

Defending the Defenders

9

Hardware and Toolsets

10

Data Analysis

11
Documentation

Part 3: Recovery – Post-Hunt Activity

12
Deliverables

13
Post-Hunt Activity and Maturing a Team

Appendix

Index

Other Books You May Enjoy

Preface

Threat hunting is a concept that takes traditional cyber defense and spins it on its head. It moves the bar for network defense beyond looking at the known threats and allows a team to pursue adversaries that are attacking in novel ways that have not previously been seen. To successfully track down and remove these advanced attackers, a solid understanding of the foundational concepts and requirements of the threat hunting framework is needed. Moreover, to confidently employ threat hunting in a business landscape, the same team will need to be able to customize that framework to fit a customer's particular use case.

This book breaks down the fundamental pieces of a threat hunting team, the stages of a hunt, and the process that needs to be followed through planning, execution, and recovery. It will take you through the process of threat hunting, starting from establishing a common understanding of cybersecurity basics that applies to almost any organization through to the in-depth requirements of building a mature hunting capability. This is provided through written instructions as well as multiple story-driven scenarios that show the correct (and incorrect) way to effectively conduct a threat hunt.

By the end of this cyber threat hunting book, you'll be able to identify the processes of handicapping an immature cyber threat hunt team and systematically progress the hunting capabilities to maturity.

Who this book is for

This book is for anyone interested in learning how to organize and execute effective cyber threat hunts, establishing extra defense capabilities within their company, and wanting to mature an organization's cybersecurity posture. It will also be useful for anyone looking for a framework to help a hunt team grow and evolve.

What this book covers

Chapter 1, An Introduction to Threat Hunting, introduces you to the concept of threat hunting and how it fits into an organization's cybersecurity structure. This information will allow everyone to begin their journey from the same starting point and remove any preconceived notions of what threat hunting is and is not.

Chapter 2, Requirements and Motivations, covers how to identify how and where threat hunting could fit into an organization's priorities and requirements. While this type of cyber defense function is important, it may not fit your organization's business priorities.

Chapter 3, Team Construct, covers the required roles and responsibilities of the various members that make up a threat hunting team. Regardless of whether the team is made up of a single individual or 20, the same basic roles must be fulfilled.

Chapter 4, Communication Breakdown, covers all of the communication methods and requirements throughout the life cycle of a threat hunt. This fundamental concept is where many teams falter, causing chaos and uncertainty to take a foothold throughout the mission.

Chapter 5, Methodologies, covers various methodologies and processes that teams should employ throughout the life cycle of a hunt. This will enable the team to have an understandable, repeatable process that they will be able to grow from.

Chapter 6, Threat Intelligence, covers one of the most overlooked areas of a threat hunt, which is the inclusion of threat intelligence.

Chapter 7, Planning, covers all of the phases and considerations of a threat hunting planning cycle. Many phases can be easily prepared ahead of time, while some will need to be finely tuned to each mission.

Chapter 8, Defending the Defenders, teaches you how to protect your customer and yourself from the malicious intentions of the adversary that's being hunted. There are numerous ways a hunt introduces risk to a network, and precautions need to be taken ahead of time to ensure that risk is mitigated.

Chapter 9, Hardware and Toolsets, talks you through the tools that threat hunters need to accomplish a hunt. These tools are both hardware and software, with a myriad of available options. The network requirements drive which tools can be used, and customer requirements will inform which tools are allowed.

Chapter 10, Data Analysis, covers data analysis. Data analysis doesn't begin and end with an analyst looking at a screen. Data must ultimately be collected, prepared, and reviewed by a human. Automation of data review is the cornerstone of a mature threat hunting team, because it allows more time for humans to find something interesting. Communicating data requirements, discoveries, and challenges is also vital to a mature team.

Chapter 11, Documentation, covers the importance of proper documentation and how it plays into every facet of a hunt as this is the only communication mechanism the team employs which will exist well beyond the hunts conclusion. Documentation internal to the team and with the mission partner will establish the boundaries and expectations needed to ensure all involved parties' requirements can be met.

Chapter 12, Deliverables, covers the types of deliverables and their methods of delivery that are normally produced in the life cycle of a threat hunt. This is where a team will truly stand out to all stakeholders within an organization as these items will continue to tell the hunting story long after all of the members have moved on to other things.

Chapter 13, Post-Hunt Activity and Maturing a Team, covers all of the events and activities that should be conducted when wrapping up a hunt but are easily forgotten by an immature or busy team. These are just a few areas that will allow a team to identify weak points and grow a collection of people into a finely tuned threat hunting capability.

Appendix, is intended to be a reference for the rest of the book that will allow you to quickly identify any items not fully understood. Additionally, sample checklists and playbooks discussed throughout the book can be found here.

To get the most out of this book

While this book walks you through the foundational concepts needed for an effective hunt team to operate, there are some prerequisites before beginning. There are three main areas that you should have an entry-level understanding of before progressing:

- Foundational concepts of cybersecurity, including organizational constructs and the impacts of poor security practices. For more information on this, refer to NIST SP 800-160 Volume 2 Revision 1 (`https://nvlpubs.nist.gov/nistpubs/SpecialPublications/NIST.SP.800-160v2r1.pdf`).

- Fundamental concepts of technical leadership and its difference from general process management.

- Information technology fundamentals allowing you to identify core concepts such as an enterprise, firewall, network traffic, and workstations versus infrastructure devices.

Download the color images

We also provide a PDF file that has color images of the screenshots and diagrams used in this book. You can download it here: `https://static.packt-cdn.com/downloads/9781803242996_ColorImages.pdf`.

Conventions used

The following convention is used throughout this book.

> **Tips or Important Notes**
> Appear like this.

Get in touch

Feedback from our readers is always welcome.

General feedback: If you have questions about any aspect of this book, email us at `customercare@packtpub.com` and mention the book title in the subject of your message.

Errata: Although we have taken every care to ensure the accuracy of our content, mistakes do happen. If you have found a mistake in this book, we would be grateful if you would report this to us. Please visit `www.packtpub.com/support/errata` and fill in the form.

Piracy: If you come across any illegal copies of our works in any form on the internet, we would be grateful if you would provide us with the location address or website name. Please contact us at `copyright@packt.com` with a link to the material.

If you are interested in becoming an author: If there is a topic that you have expertise in and you are interested in either writing or contributing to a book, please visit `authors.packtpub.com`.

Share Your Thoughts

Once you've read *The Foundations of Threat Hunting,* we'd love to hear your thoughts! Scan the QR code below to go straight to the Amazon review page for this book and share your feedback.

https://packt.link/r/180324299-X

Your review is important to us and the tech community and will help us make sure we're delivering excellent quality content.

Part 1: Preparation – Why and How to Start the Hunting Process

Here, you will gain an understanding of why an organization should or should not hunt and how to start that process.

This part of the book comprises the following chapters:

- *Chapter 1, An Introduction to Threat Hunting*
- *Chapter 2, Requirements and Motivations*
- *Chapter 3, Team Construct*
- *Chapter 4, Communication Breakdown*
- *Chapter 5, Methodologies*
- *Chapter 6, Threat Intelligence*
- *Chapter 7, Planning*

1
An Introduction to Threat Hunting

Threat hunting is a concept that can bring to mind a myriad of different images and ideas. It is a concept that is shrouded in mystery for some, while others might have been able to hone it down to a science, perhaps going as far as applying their findings in new ways. The line that separates these two groups is an understanding that this idea of hunting is, in reality, a loosely based concept that is molded for each unique situation, environment, and the personnel involved.

In the event that you have not heard of this concept of threat hunting before, it is very helpful to understand that there is not a single cookie-cutter cybersecurity solution for any network, enterprise, or incident. A single solution simply does not and cannot exist. There are millions of variables and conditions, both technical and organizational, that will differentiate one organization's network from another. The simple appearance of security might be a deterrent for some adversaries against a target and a challenge to others.

Even if an organization does all of the correct steps, such as ensuring that the network is architected with proper layered defenses, vulnerabilities are thoroughly analyzed, and risks are minimized, there are still important protections to enforce. A continual improvement process must be in place to review all the previous findings to see how the environment has changed. Threat hunting is a critical part of that process for organizations looking to mature their cybersecurity posture and improve their resilience in the digital world.

Of the countless threat hunting events we have had the pleasure of taking part in or observing, no two were ever the same. Each hunt was tailored to the particular technical resources available, enterprise in question, perceived threat, personnel assigned, and business requirements of the client. The aim of this book is to provide you with foundational concepts and requirements needed to take a generic threat hunting framework and mold it into something that will fit a particular use case that a customer would be willing to accept based upon what they are experiencing. This framework will allow you to understand how to build a threat hunting team and define and respond in future hunts to meet business needs while minimizing resource waste and non-value-added efforts.

In this chapter, we will be covering the following topics

- Incident response life cycle
- Why is threat hunting important?
- Application of detection levels
- Book layout

By the end of this chapter, you will be able to do the following:

- *Comprehend* the difference between cyber threat hunting and other types of cyber defense functions.
- *Discuss* how threat hunting fits into the NIST incident response life cycle.
- *Comprehend* the importance of conducting effective threat hunting missions.

Incident response life cycle (hunting as proactive detection)

There are numerous different incident response life cycles that can be found through a short search across the internet. To keep things simple, any time this book references the incident response life cycle, it will be alluding to the one found in the following diagram:

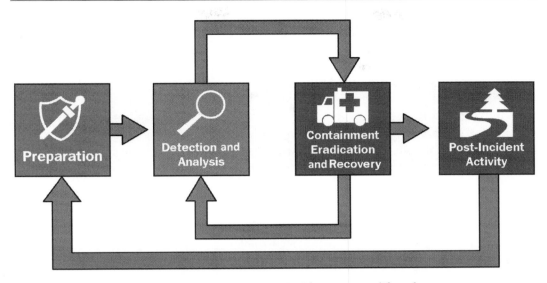

Figure 1.1 – NIST SP 800-61r2 incident response life cycle

The cycle always starts out with a *Preparation* phase, regardless of whether it is done purposefully or not. The following two steps, *Detection and Analysis* and *Containment, Eradication, and Recovery*, are cycled between as new information is identified and cases expanded. Once everything has been recovered, there will be a *Post-Incident Activity* phase in which a review of the events can be conducted without any pressure to recover. Good practices can be encouraged and bad practices pruned. Let's take a closer look at each of these phases.

Preparation

Plan for incidents, document assets and actions, architect for secure solutions, baseline the network, and so on. This is where an organization will prepare for the employment of cybersecurity resources. Even if they completely outsource their risk and response to another entity, the owning organization will take part in this phase. There will always be a level of preparation completed; sometimes it just happens to be that the organization decides not to prepare at all.

Some such examples of activities found within this phase include measuring baseline network activity, reviewing and documenting standard processes, and stress testing response scenarios. For example, if a virus was found on a network, how would the administrators respond? Preparation would allow them to understand the best course of action in relation to the business priorities that would allow them to minimize risk to the organization and its priorities. With inadequate preparation, the next few phases will be purely responsive with a higher level of risk to the organization.

Detection and analysis

During this phase, the organization will identify what is perceived to be benign and what is potentially malicious. This includes detection of activity, analysis of that activity, and a full-scope investigation as needed to determine the root cause and scope of the event. Cyber threat hunting is only a part of this step. The threat hunting step can be iterated over and over before a vulnerability or incident is identified that requires containment, eradication, and recovery. It does well to understand that this phase does not have to be completed by the organization that owns the network. Detection of an event can come from any number of places, including government agencies, hacktivists, underground hacking forums, and news sites.

Some examples of activities found within this phase include monitoring antivirus and firewall lows, comparison of baseline network activity against current network activity, and threat hunting. Anything that brings a particular activity to the focus of a cyber defender could fall under this phase of the cycle.

Containment, eradication, and recovery

Slow down, remove, and recover from the realization of a vulnerability that was exploited. The overarching goal is for the enterprise and organization to leave this phase operating at whatever the previously defined concept of *normal* was. This phase is largely dependent upon the planning that was conducted during the first phase because it will outline the methods in which the recovery activities are executed. If these actions were not properly planned or completed poorly during the first phase, then this phase will be an extreme struggle in a time of already heightened stress. One item of note is that it is expected for the middle phases of this life cycle to loop back and forth as new information is identified and additional pieces of the puzzle on the adversary are put into place. There will be a clear stopping point: all key data points have been identified and recovered from or all funds for the incident have been expended.

This phase is dependent upon the thoroughness of the previous phase. Some example activities include the locking of accounts, the implementation of additional firewall rules, and having users retake cybersecurity awareness training. Any activity that helps reset the network back to the previous *baseline* without the offending action could be included in this phase. Many of the organizational-level activities that occur in this phase will be outside the scope of a traditional threat hunting team.

Post-incident activity

This phase is intended to ensure that the risk is removed and the vulnerability is not exploited again. Within this phase, the organization will attempt to learn from the incident that occurred and the recovery that took place. Unfortunately, at this point, the organization and defenders are normally tired of the whole event and want to be done. This phase is the most overlooked and underaccomplished of the four phases, which explains why many organizations are compromised in the same way repeatedly. Everyone must learn from the correct and incorrect things that occurred in order to not repeat the mistakes of the past. Failure to do so is inviting those same things to happen again to the detriment of the organization.

Some examples of activities that take place include the incident response debrief for an intrusion and the reviewing of patching policies. Many of the organizational-level activities that occur in this phase will be outside the scope of a traditional threat hunting team.

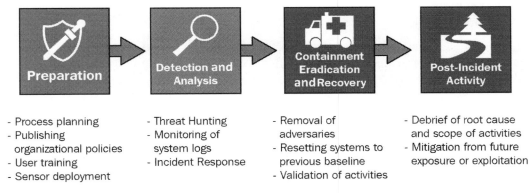

Figure 1.2 – Sample activities that occur in each phase

There are many activities that can occur in each phase of the incident response life cycle with stakeholders taking part in some or all of the phases. The most important takeaway to have when working through this cycle is to understand which phase you are in and what you are intending to accomplish. Follow the process and employ the correct teams and personnel as needed. If an adversary is just discovered, do not jump ahead and attempt to begin the removal of any artifacts that are found.

Why is threat hunting important?

Reactive detection methods, such as utilizing signatures of known malicious files (hashes) or monitoring for behaviors synonymous with an attack (heuristics), can fail for a number of reasons. Detection based on known hashes can easily fail as it is simple to change a known malicious file just enough to bypass standard and even advanced antivirus solutions. Any free hex editor can be used to modify a file with a single bit and bypass this defense. Heuristics can also fail as they rely on *known* bad behaviors while attempting to account for expected administration behavior on the network. This does little for the unknown bad behaviors that are evolving in the threat actors' environments.

Taking the opposite approach and *whitelisting* known good behavior and applications is a method that an enterprise can take to create a *zero-trust environment*. The truth behind this concept is that very few organizations can and should fully implement this type of construct. This method is extremely resource-intensive to deploy across an enterprise while keeping services up to date as software and people change. Even then, someone who is masquerading as a legit user following that user's normal behavior could operate under the defense's thresholds.

A proactive detection method such as threat hunting doesn't wait for an alert and doesn't require the administrative overhead to whitelist all approved actions. Threat hunting takes into account the current vulnerabilities, environment, and processes to apply human expertise against the evidence. Threat hunting allows an organization to apply a force multiplier to their cybersecurity processes by augmenting the automated and administrated defenses.

Another reason why threat hunting is important is that it provides a focus for cybersecurity that is from an entirely different **point of view** (**POV**) than is normally found in a **Security Operations Center** (**SOC**). This different POV eschews the alarms and tools associated with them. Threat hunting wants to look directly at the evidence on the endpoints to determine whether there was some activity that was missed or the SOC tools haven't been updated to detect.

While there are many different methods of detecting adversarial behavior on a network, they can all be put into one of two categories – reactive or proactive. Think of reactive detection like a building alarm that is triggered when a window is opened. Once triggered, security will go and investigate what happened and why that window was opened. Proactive detection, of which threat hunting is one method of detection, does not wait for an alarm to go off. Using the same analogy, this would be a security guard who patrols the building looking for unlocked windows even though no alarms have gone off.

The following is a real-world example:

- **Location**: High-security facility.

- **Reaction detection methods**: Alarms on doors and windows; each door is automatically secured with a locking mechanism; entry is protected by a radio frequency identification (RFID) badging in/out system; motion detectors for after business hours or in restricted/unoccupied spaces.

- **Behavior (heuristics) tracking methods**: Each individual is issued an RFID picture badge to scan into the facility and enter restricted spaces. Members have unique accounts to log in to systems that track what system or resource was accessed at a specific time.

- **Proactive detection methods**: Security guards will patrol the building and review access/personnel for abnormal or malicious activity and stop random individuals for security checks of bags and accesses. If anything appears out of the ordinary, the security guards have the authority to intervene and review the facts around the particular event before allowing it to continue further.

Without this *proactive detection method* employed across the building, any activity that mimics an insider or unknown threat would be almost impossible to detect.

> Definition
>
> **True positive**: An alert that is triggered by reactive defenses that is valid, in that it meets the intent of the signature or heuristics for which it triggered, for example, an antivirus signature alert of a trojan that was downloaded.
>
> **True negative**: The lack of a trigger by reactive defenses during the analysis of normal and expected system behavior or communications.
>
> **False positive**: An alert that is triggered by reactive defenses that is invalid, meaning that it does not meet the intent of the signature or heuristics for which it triggered, for example, an intrusion prevention system firing on someone searching the internet for testmyids.com.
>
> **False negative**: The lack of a trigger by reactive defenses on abnormal or malicious system behavior or communications during analysis, for example, an adversary emulating an administrator in order to successfully exfiltrate data from the network.

Application of detection levels

Incident response and SOC teams will usually be concerned with having *low false positive* rates. Remember that these are the alarms that are triggered even though nothing malicious actually occurred. Having a false positive rate that is low will help ensure that any alarms that fire and are brought to the SOC analyst's attention are a true concern. The reason for this is that evaluating and investigating a false positive can cause a massive drain on the incident response or SOC resources. Investigating an alarm that is not malicious in nature and actually a benign activity does not provide any improvement to network defenses. The trade-off for focusing on a low false positive rate is that there will be a *higher level of false negatives* due to the higher requirements for alerts to trigger. This, in turn, means that there will be a higher percentage of activity that is malicious in nature but will not trigger any alarms.

A threat hunter is concerned with the inverse of SOC requirements. When setting the bar for what is considered anomalous and requiring further investigation, the threat hunting team accepts having a *high false positive* rate. High false positives will help ensure that the respective false negatives are *kept very low*. A threat hunting team can accept a high false positive rate due to the scope of their hunt being very narrow compared to the scope an SOC would be monitoring on a day-to-day basis.

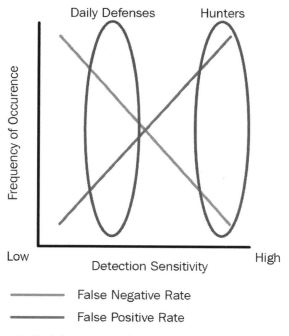

Figure 1.3 – Daily defenses versus hunt team heuristic sensitivity threshold

The preceding diagram depicts this consideration of false negative versus false positive. For a business just getting into threat hunting, this could mean a paradigm shift for parts of their team in how they measure success on a daily basis. An example would be an organization that uses the false positive rate as a measurement of success. For daily defenses, this will normally be tuned so that it is low, thus enabling the front-line cyber defenders to focus only on the things that truly matter and not waste time with dead ends. When the organization starts hunting and needs to measure their success, the false positive rate for a hunt team should be very high. Leadership looking at those statistics might be *trained* to think that this is a bad thing when, in fact, it is expected.

Book layout

This book is laid out in a manner intended to help you better prepare for and understand the contents of each chapter. Each chapter will have five sections:

- **Introduction and learning outcomes**: This area will introduce you to the main focus of the chapter, as well as outlining the expected high-level areas that you should remember as you review the material. Each learning objective will start with one of the following three words:

    - If the objective starts with *Identify*, then the intention is just for you to have a higher-level understanding of the topic. You do not need to worry about having an expert-level understanding of that material.

    - If the objective starts with *Comprehend*, then the intention is for you to be able to apply the topic and extrapolate how it would fit into a given scenario.

    - If the objective starts with *Discuss*, then the intention is for you to be able to have an educated discussion with another knowledgeable person on the topic. Not only would you fully understand the concept, but you would also be able to apply it in real time to various scenarios.

- **Topic focus**: This area is the main focus of the chapter and will provide all of the details needed for you to understand the topic.

- **Scenarios**: This area is broken up into two fictional subscenarios, one focused on an internal hunt team and one focused on an external hunt team. The internal hunt team is one that exists full time within the scenario's organization. The external hunt team is a team that was contracted out by the scenario's organization to perform a specific threat hunt. These scenarios will build upon the previous chapter's scenario.

- **Summary**: This area will provide you with a summary of the chapter and any higher-level takeaways that you should continue to focus on.

- **Review questions**: This area will provide you with a chance to test your understanding of the material through a few questions or scenarios aimed at reinforcing the learning objectives stated at the beginning of the chapter.

This structure should help you go through and understand the content of each chapter, and the book at large, in the most efficient manner.

Summary

In review, understanding the difference between threat hunting and other forms of cyber defense will be critical for your journey forward. Most cybersecurity defenses are reactive in nature, in that they act as an alarm that is triggered on a known bad event. Unlike many *standard* defense mechanisms found across networks, cyber threat hunting is a proactive defense mechanism in that it is executed without any warning or indication of malicious activity. With all of that in mind, cyber threat hunting can still be a part of the incident response life cycle.

It is able to do so by providing an additional layer of dynamic and proactive security onto the standard reactive defense mechanisms commonly employed by enterprises. This proactive defense concept is not new and can be found in many organizations' physical security elements. One of the main differences that defenders identify with is that day-to-day defenders will thrive in an environment with a low false positive rate in order to not waste resources. Threat hunters will want a low false negative rate in order to ensure nothing slips past their investigation.

Without proactive defenses, there will be a distinctive limit to what can be achieved in the realm of security. Many *advanced* technics and adversaries could easily slip past reactive defenses and wreak havoc before being detected.

Now that we know what cyber threat hunting is, we will look at the *whys* and *hows* for identifying what is needed for a cyber threat hunt in the next chapter.

Review questions

Answer the following questions to check your knowledge of this chapter:

1. (True or false) Cyber threat hunting is reactive in nature.

2. The NIST incident response life cycle is made up of which four stages?

   A. Preparation, Detection and Analysis, Re-Baselining Systems, Policy Alignment

   B. Planning, Preparation, Detection, Recovery

   C. Preparation, Detection and Analysis, Containment, Eradication, and Recovery, Post-Incident Activity

   D. Planning, Detection, Containment, Post-Incident Activity

3. Threat hunting is mainly a part of which phase of the NIST incident response life cycle?

4. (True or false) Threat hunting is unique to cyber defense.

5. (Insert the correct answer) Steady-state defenses such as incident response will normally want low _____ _____ rates. Threat hunters will normally want high _____ _____ rates.

   - False positive

   - True positive

   - False negative

   - True negative

Review answers

The answers to the review questions are as follows:

1. False. Cyber threat hunting is proactive as the hunter does not wait for an alarm or alert before searching for malicious behavior.

2. C. See NIST SP 800-61r2 incident response life cycle.

3. Detection and Analysis. See NIST SP 800-61r2 incident response life cycle.

4. False. The threat hunting concept is used in many different fields.

5. False positive; False negative. See the *Application of detection levels* section of this chapter.

2
Requirements and Motivations

There are numerous reasons an organization might feel compelled to invest resources in a cyber threat hunting team. The motivations for a business will vary depending on the sector they operate in, organizational size, and reliance on IT. However, for a business, there are very few events as motivating as identifying a risk with a high probability of occurrence that also carries with it significant legal and financial repercussions.

When the risk materializes, the organization's preparation and existing defenses will be the deciding factor on the length, breadth, and depth of the compromise that occurs. The employment of a cyber threat hunting team will help severely shorten the time window an adversary has to cause havoc in an enterprise. When the smoke clears, depending upon the regulatory bodies or laws the organization follows, questions might be asked about whether everything that should have been done was. There are also legal requirements that could include the reporting of the incident to law enforcement or organizational stakeholders (investors, partners, and so on). Finally, if there is any insurance involved, claims will be reviewed against what the business did to protect itself before the attack. If there were glaring errors in the cybersecurity decisions made before the incident, then payouts may be in jeopardy.

> **Important Note**
>
> If you have not heard the saying before, take the following to heart: It is not a matter of *if*, rather *when* your organization will be compromised.

In this chapter, the following topics will be covered:

- Regulatory requirements, legalities, and best practices – where to start…
- Why do you want to conduct threat hunts?
- Internal versus external teams
- What is needed to conduct a successful threat hunt?
- Types of threat hunts
- Scopes of threat hunts
- Scenario A—internal threat hunt
- Scenario B—external threat hunt

By the end of this chapter, you will be able to do the following:

- *Identify* the difference between regulatory requirements, organizational standards, and best practices as they apply to a proposed threat hunt.
- *Comprehend* the individual and organizational benefits of conducting a threat hunt.
- *Comprehend* whether to utilize an external or internal hunt team.
- *Discuss* the differences between the various types of cyber threat hunt requirements.

Regulatory requirements, legalities, and best practices – where to start...

While threat hunting is one of the best ways to identify malicious activity with a high return on investment for an organization, there are many other reasons to employ this style of cyber defense in an enterprise. One of the biggest drives for an organization to do this is when organizational leadership says *we have to*. Yes, but why? Has the organization established its own internal standards or policies that state how often and why it would employ this method of cyber defense? If so, then it would be entirely internally driven and an internal business decision on whether or not to continue to follow that policy. All of the external causes for building a threat hunting team require the same thing: due diligence. While standards, laws, or insurance contracts won't directly say *that an organization must "stand up a cyber threat hunting team"*, they will say things such as *implement best practices for cybersecurity* or *ensure cybersecurity controls are tested at a certain frequency*. Insurance payouts will depend on showing no negligence on the part of stakeholders. Attorneys for the state as well as stakeholders (for example, investors) will also want to ensure that enterprise leadership did their due diligence to secure the environment.

Maybe the organization is following an external requirement as found in any of the various regulations, such as the **Payment Card Industry Data Security Standard** (**PCI DSS**), the Sarbanes-Oxley Act or the **General Data Protection Regulation** (**GDPR**). Regulations and laws at this level are above the authority of the organization to decide whether or not to follow. Additionally, these laws are growing in regulatory power and expanding across the globe. If the regulations and laws are not properly adhered to, then it may be extremely costly to the organization. This cost could be a monetary fine or lawsuit, or via the loss of experienced leadership due to removal for possible prosecution.

Many organizations have entire departments dedicated to identifying, monitoring, and tracking these very things, yet it can still be overwhelming for a team or individual to fully understand what the organization has prioritized its resources toward. Thankfully, there is a relatively simple process that anyone could follow to gain a better understanding of what an organization most likely cares about and subsequently should be adhering to. Look no further than the **National Institute of Standards and Technology (NIST)**'s updated **Cyber Security Framework (CSF)**. This framework can be found on the NIST website (`https://www.nist.gov/cyberframework`).

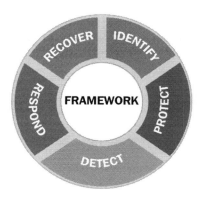

Figure 2.1 – CSF version 1.1

Reprinted courtesy of the National Institute of Standards and Technology, U.S. Department of Commerce. Not copyrightable in the United States.

For anyone who is part of an organization that wants to improve but is not sure where to begin, this framework is for you, and it is an amazing resource. At the framework's center, it breaks up the concept of cybersecurity into five core functions: **identify**, **protect**, **detect**, **respond**, and **recover**. Each function is broken up into categories that go into more specific subcategories that each have references that might apply to your organization. The intention of the CSF is not for people to utilize it as a checklist, but rather as a guide to managing cybersecurity risk within their organization. Additionally, it should be used on top of an organizational framework and complement existing practices, not be put in place of them.

The Framework provides a common language for understanding, managing, and expressing cybersecurity risk to internal and external stakeholders. It can be used to help identify and prioritize actions for reducing cybersecurity risk, and it is a tool for aligning policy, business, and technological approaches to managing that risk.

NIST (2018) Framework for Improving Critical Infrastructure Cybersecurity

The CSF guides the reader through identifying what the organization's cybersecurity posture maturity currently is, setting goals, scoping where they want or need to be, prioritizing improvements, and communicating with applicable stakeholders in the appropriate business languages. For some organizations, when conducting a review of the framework against business needs, stakeholders may identify priorities that result in threat hunting not being an important cybersecurity requirement at that time. This is *OK* and can be a win for the organization as they are able to appropriately invest their resources in areas needing further investment that are aligned with their organizational goals, risk profile, and cybersecurity maturity requirements. Whether or not you end up conducting threat hunts, this framework will be worthwhile for any organization: employ it early and review it often.

Regulatory or legal requirements are dependent on the purpose of the organization and the environment it operates in. The United States federal government has been developing better assets to assist organizations with cybersecurity concerns. One of the best assets is the **Multi-State Information Sharing and Analysis Center** (**MS-ISAC**), funded by the Department of Homeland Security through CISA, which can be found here: `https://www.cisecurity.org/ms-isac/`. MS-ISAC has resources to identify what organizational requirements there are legally for when a breach happens.

Why do you want to conduct threat hunts?

Moving beyond organizational priorities and regulatory adherence, there are additional reasons why conducting threat hunts is extremely beneficial. From a business perspective, a cyber threat hunt can lead to a quick win for cybersecurity leadership due to reducing the number of risks that are unknowingly accepted by managers, decreasing the time the **Security Operations Center** (**SOC**) spends searching through false positive alerts, and saving money due to mitigating vulnerabilities before a breach. 20 years ago, a business might have been able to get away with having a minimal, if any, computer footprint. Today, not utilizing computers in business is impossible to do, ensuring that a threat actor's target will always be present. It is not possible to completely obstruct threat actors wanting to exploit those targets because those threat actors are completely outside of organizational control and not all targets are known. The only way to manage these unknown targets, also known as risks, that reactive defenses cannot detect is to systematically look for them, which is exactly what threat hunting does!

For those individuals in enterprises who manage and defend these risky networks on a day-by-day basis, threat hunting can provide valuable insight into what the full scope of the cyberspace terrain actually is. It is one thing to say the organization's network environment was designed a certain way, and another to see it in action and understand how things are actually interacting. Network managers with a good amount of experience have run into the scenario where a system was supposed to be configured one way but wasn't due to an accidental or undocumented configuration change, or a rogue employee (or division) taking it upon themselves to *improve* the network. This is known as *shadow IT*; it is believing a network is configured or deployed in one manner but in reality, it exists in a completely separate way. *Shadow IT* is a real threat with unknown vulnerabilities and risks for all organizations. These are examples of some of the types of vulnerabilities that an adversary will take advantage of regardless of the root cause of its existence.

Additionally, while not necessarily the most exciting part of a threat hunt, a massive amount of documentation on organizational best practices and baseline behavior can be generated. One of the underlying goals for conducting cyber threat hunts in an organization should always be to either update and validate the existing baseline knowledge or begin the generation of current documentation. The baseline documentation should include input from both passive and active data collectors spread across the network.

This documentation assists the network managers of the organization since the scope of the cyberspace environment can finally be definitively proven and current protection measures can be verified. Managers and developers also benefit from this baseline, creating or updating, as the findings can be used as clear evidence for where additional cybersecurity investment needs to occur or where organizationally unacceptable risks have been tacitly accepted. Any sliver of knowledge that can provide an organization with better insight into their environment makes future risk management decisions easier and more appropriate for the organization.

The following are individual and team-level benefits to threat hunting:

- Turns unknown risks into known risks and allows them to be managed effectively
- Identifies adversarial activities that made it through existing defenses
- Provides an increased understanding of what threats current defenses have visibility into and where those defenses could be lacking
- Increases understanding of the enterprise for all personnel involved
- Validates/develops a documented network baseline and map
- Provides insight into potential system and network misconfigurations
- Identifies gaps in logging and network visibility

The following are (higher-level) organizational benefits to threat hunting:

- Improves adherence to legal and regulatory requirements
- Aides in risk management decisions before or after major network reconfigurations, such as mergers with other organizations
- Validates threat intelligence reporting specific to the organization and the threat actors that are targeting them
- Can be utilized as a proof point for any investment adjustments into specific network security areas
- Re-enforces stakeholders' trust in the confidentiality, integrity, and availability of the network

With the question of *Should an organization be conducting threat hunts?* out of the way, the next big decision that any organization will need to discuss is the *how*. There are two main approaches to this; either build an internal team or outsource to another organization to perform the necessary actions. Each has its own merits and demerits that will need to be considered before a direction is firmly chosen.

Internal versus external teams

Now that an organization has decided that it is in their best interest to conduct threat hunts, the question to answer is whether they need their own team or whether it would be in their best interest to contract a third party to act as an external team. The answer to that is: well, it depends. The selection of the team will need to be based upon the business decisions that are driven by identified risks, long-term strategy, and regulatory or legal requirements. For some organizations, it is a cost-effective solution to stand up a dedicated internal threat hunt team that only focuses on organizational areas in a systematic fashion. For other organizations, they might want to bring in a team once or twice a year to satisfy a few niche business needs in critical areas only. Neither is a wrong decision. The pros and cons of each type of hunt, the requirements to perform a successful hunt, and the type of hunt that could be conducted will need to be considered. Each of these would need to be carefully aligned to ensure that it is producing a meaningful product for the organization.

The following are the pros and cons of internal teams:

Pros:

- Existing understanding of the network and organizational priorities
- Potential long-term improvement in operator knowledge of the enterprise

Cons:

- Costly to maintain a dedicated team or redirect existing employees from other tasks
- Acquisition and retention of experienced hunters
- Potential bias in knowledge and understanding of the network, leading to risks being assumed and possibly overlooked

The following are the pros and cons of external teams:

Pros:

- No network bias; the team walks in with no expectations of network configuration
- Higher-quality return on investment for short-term and specific threat hunts
- More experience due to many different client environments
- No business risk for losing technical capabilities with personnel leaving

Cons:

- Can be a higher resource cost if utilized extensively over a long period
- Can be a higher resource cost for a dedicated team
- Lack of network familiarity will lead to a preparation period, extending the timeline for engagement and cost

With a basic understanding of the differences between utilizing an internal team compared to an external team, a deeper dive into the overarching organizational constructs that must exist for that team to be successful is needed. Without these items in place, the chances for the team to be wasteful and not complete their requested objectives will dramatically increase.

What is needed to conduct a successful threat hunt?

The most basic, and most common, version of a threat hunt can be conducted by a single employee with privileges and tools who is curious about some activity. This employee must also have the appropriate authority and access to additional information on the organization and from the internet. The size and scope of the team become irrelevant when talking about the most basic requirements needed to hunt on an enterprise. A successful threat hunt requires five specific items to be there.

- **An organization that wants to have a threat hunt conducted**

  Out of all of the requirements, this is the most critical. Woe is the hunter that is tracking an adversary across an organization that does not care or wants the hunter there. Taken from experience, this always results in numerous questionable, but unverified, anomalies being found. Those anomalies are documented and reported to the organizational stakeholders who do not utilize the new information provided to them. The hunt turns into an exercise in which a compliance box is checked, validating to an auditor that a network security function was performed. The adversary achieves their objective, network security does not improve, and the organization's cyber footprint stagnates for another year.

  For a successful threat hunt, there must be willing participation across the organization. Stakeholder involvement throughout the organization's leadership is necessary for a successful hunt.

- **An organization that is willing and capable of granting the necessary access and authorities to the threat hunting team**

  Just because someone wants to do something, does not mean they can. The appropriate stakeholders in the organization will need to be able to grant the appropriate authorizations for the hunt. For internal teams, this is rarely an issue, whereas for external teams, this can be a major roadblock. There is no cookie-cutter answer for how to traverse this need. It is dependent upon the organization, its leadership's views on cybersecurity, and the laws that govern them.

  The organization must give the network access and the resources in terms of the people and tools needed. If it does not, then the hunt will not be able to produce any positive results.

- **An organization that is willing and capable of integrating the results of the threat hunt into their defenses and business processes**

Wanting and authorizing a threat hunt does not always mean an organization will conduct any meaningful follow-up with the results of the hunt. Commonly, this is the result of either a lack of understanding of how to effectively use this new information or a lack of resources to implement the necessary changes. From personal experience on both sides of the table (business stakeholder and threat hunter), it can be frustrating to see the same results from past hunts but the inability to do anything about it.

The hunt will not be successful if the organization simply takes the results and does nothing. Threat hunting is part of a successful continuous improvement process. A very simple way this can be done is to utilize the various detection methods employed by the threat hunters and have them implemented and managed in an automated fashion. The inclusion of specific keywords and strings that the threat hunting team found useful are great examples of *tailored* signatures that can be employed by the SOC to carry on their work.

- **A plan that satisfies business requirements and identifies a goal for the team to attempt to achieve**

If your team has made it this far, then the last step that is required is a plan that aligns with the business requirements. Just because the team knows that there is malware from a specific group on the network, it does not make it a priority to chase down. Ensure all members understand and align their actions with the business needs and concerns. Doing so will help ensure that regardless of what is or is not found, the hunt will be a success. The hunt team must plan accordingly. There is no hunting without planning.

Evidence that is always requested by a threat hunting team, but is not a must-have requirement, is the availability of historical data (for example, logs, and packet captures (PCAP) past 24 hours). Additionally, it is not a requirement for a specific security posture to already be in place within the organization (for example, defenses and sensors already in place). These artifacts or orientations are always extremely helpful and aid in the execution of a threat hunt. In *Chapter 12, Deliverables*, we delve into assessment confidence levels that will be greatly influenced by the inclusion or absence of these items. But you don't need them to get started!

- **A threat hunting team with the appropriate processes, training, and equipment**

  To put it plainly, just because someone is called a threat hunter, does not make them one. They will need the appropriate mindset and tactics, techniques, and procedures to get them started in the right direction. The team needs to know how to hunt; even if inexperienced, there are easy tools and instructions on how to do a first hunt.

Depending upon the experience level of the team and the maturity of the target organization, there are four different *types* of hunts that are typically conducted. Now that we have an understanding of what is required to conduct a successful threat hunt, let's explore the different types of hunts that are normally conducted.

Types of threat hunts

There are *technically* four distinct categories of threat hunts that can be conducted. These are all based upon two main factors-the amount of information known about the adversary (intelligence) and the amount of information known about the targeted network (network knowledge).

> **Definitions**
>
> **Intelligence**: The level of understanding about the adversary the organization is concerned about
>
> **Network knowledge**: The level of detailed understanding of the target network

Four different categories of threat hunts are possible:

- **Low intelligence/low network knowledge**: A review of data is provided, which could end up being random artifacts unrelated to each other, requiring the establishment of a *pseudo* network baseline. Do not do this as it is not repeatable! While it can be fun for an individual, it will be driven by the personality of the hunter whether or not the organization benefits from the resources expended.

- **High intelligence/low network knowledge**: An intel-based hunt that requires the establishment of a *pseudo* network baseline. This is the common category hunt type for external teams contracted by the organization. Effectiveness improves as the owning organization's cybersecurity stance matures and baseline documents are available for the hunt.

- **Low intelligence/high network knowledge**: A behavioral-based hunt where a baseline exists in some form with no specific adversary or attack vector in mind instead of looking for deviations from the true baseline. This can be done with a well-documented network or based upon input from individuals with a high understanding of the enterprise.

- **High intelligence/high network knowledge**: An indicator of compromise (IOC)/anomaly-based hunt where a true baseline exists and can be compared against an existing activity with a specific adversary and/or attack vector in mind. Capable only when an organization heavily invests resources into cybersecurity.

These four categories could be presented in a quad chart to better depict how they are aligned. A hunt might not firmly land in one of the quadrants; instead, they might align more to one side. This is fine and completely expected. The end goal is to provide an understanding of where things are starting off and set the level of expectations with all stakeholders. If there is low network knowledge with a low intelligence level, all individuals involved should understand that the hunt will be very broad in nature, and answering very targeted questions would not be possible.

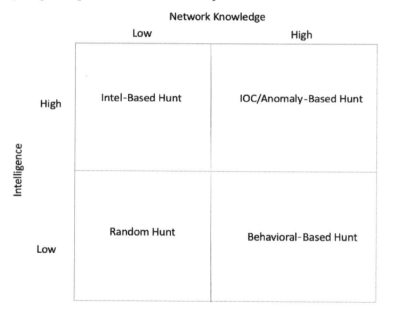

Figure 2.2 – Threat hunting category quad chart

There are some considerations to be made when it comes to measuring intelligence for a hunt. Answering these items will help increase the perceived level of intelligence throughout the hunt life cycle:

- Can it be narrowed down to a specific threat actor?

- Can it be narrowed down to specific attack capabilities or techniques?

- Can it be narrowed down to a level of sophistication?

Intelligence-level examples are as follows:

- *Low intelligence* would be the equivalent of saying we are worried about bad people. By not specifying any indicators or actors, a defender is left to look for anything that they consider *bad*.

- *High intelligence* would be utilizing a threat report on a specific actor and utilizing the MITRE ATT&CK matrix in a purposeful way to focus the threat hunt.

When measuring the level of network knowledge, there are different questions that should be presented to the stakeholders for consideration. While the hunt team could produce some of these items during their time on the network, they could never fully replace a mature organization that has a firm understanding of its own environment:

- Does a network map (traffic flow, configuration) exist?

- Is there a standard configuration and naming convention that is utilized throughout the environment?

- Are trust zones adhered to with only documented exceptions?

- Are account behaviors tracked and logged in a manner that they can be reviewed at a later time?

Network knowledge-level examples are as follows:

- *Low network knowledge* can be associated with an organization's network, providing very little (or outdated, or any) network maps, baseline configurations, and expected activity. This will cause the team to have to build their own *baseline* of current configuration that would have to be slowly validated throughout the threat hunting process and may miss areas not investigated.

- *High network knowledge* could be achieved by an organization that could provide detailed network maps, baseline system configurations, and expected account behaviors, which would speed up the planning phases of the hunt.

From here, the team will need to move on to a deeper discussion with the target organization concerning what they will be focused on. This is referred to as *scope*. Without a proper scope, the expectations for what the hunt will attempt to accomplish will have a good chance of being misaligned with what is possible while leaving the door open for massive disappointment for all members involved.

Scopes of threat hunts

The scope or the size of the threat hunt is based upon realistic constraints and restraints that exist for the situation.

> **Definitions**
>
> **Constraint**: A limitation or restriction put on by an outside force or entity. This includes those by higher-level organizations and legal or regulatory authorities.
>
> **Restraint**: A limitation or restriction put on by an internal force or entity. These include restraints from internal organizational stakeholders and policy, or the hunt team.

Limited resources

Time, equipment, personnel, access. All of these things will factor into how much can be accomplished in accordance with the business requirements of the organization.

Network size

Narrow, targeted scopes are needed for larger networks. If a team is hunting across 1 million node networks without sensors predeployed across the enterprise, a good portion of their time might be spent deploying and tuning the equipment. So, plan accordingly.

Assumed limitations

Multiple hunts can be conducted if the organization is willing to dedicate resources to the effort. The first hunt could be focused on four specific threat vectors, after which the SOC defenders could automate observing those indicators. Then the hunt team would focus on another four threat vectors, and so on.

Limited team size

A general good practice is to keep teams (or cells) limited to five or six individuals. A single hunt could be comprised of multiple cells to increase their throughput of data, network size, or targets during the hunt. The size of the team must always be tailored to the requirements of the hunt.

For example, a threat hunt on a small network of 5,000 systems with a limited amount of traffic and only a few weeks' worth of data to focus on could probably be accomplished by one or two personnel. Instead, if there were a network of over 1 million systems, a few dozen enclaves, and terabytes of data moving into and out of the network each day, then two or three teams might be needed to cover all of the areas thoroughly. Remember, there is no one right answer; each hunt will be unique and require its own perspective on what the requirements are.

Gauging and limited throughput for the team

The throughput for each team will have to be gauged on a case-by-case basis. A hypothetical team of six personnel comprised of experienced analysts could notionally handle up to four different hypotheses for an IOC-based hunt on a 100,000-node network over the course of 2 weeks if all required datasets were readily available. The same team with half of the personnel being inexperienced might need to cut the number of hypotheses in half to meet the same timeline.

We will cover what hypotheses are and how to generate them in *Chapter 5, Methodologies*.

Scenario A – internal threat hunt

The **Federal Bureau of Investigation** (**FBI**) notified Widget Maker Inc's management of a phishing campaign targeting several employees at strategic business locations globally. The investigator explained that a foreign entity began a campaign 4 months ago targeting companies within the United States with government contracts to build advanced artificial intelligence capabilities. They also stated several systems within the company's public address space had been sending beaconing network traffic to a known command and control server associated with the campaign.

With the company's intellectual property at stake, the **Chief Executive Officer (CEO)** authorized the establishment of a permanent threat hunting team utilizing internal resources from the SOC and **Network Operations Center (NOC)**. With the knowledge of subject matter experts, the data provided by the FBI, and intelligence gained through open source intelligence, the threat hunting team conducted their inaugural hunt based on the high intelligence/high network knowledge construct. The CEO authorized an experienced leader within the SOC to hand-select five existing members in the organization in order to establish this new defensive capability. They were able to utilize a dedicated working environment for their daily activities' but had a very limited budget for purchasing new capabilities.

During the team leader's onboarding discussion with the organization's senior leadership, they were able to lay out the team's initial priorities to focus on: the top priority was to enhance all defenses for their intellectual property with a focus on those associated with government controls and artificial intelligence. While any threat was of interest to the organization, they were mainly interested in the adversary that was posing a threat to their long-term stability.

Scenario B – external threat hunt

A new threat hunting team, Cyber Sleuths International, was making waves across the cyber defense community. What started out as a four-person organization with nothing more than a few laptops and good ideas steadily grew into a mature organization that provided cyber defense services around the globe. This leap from backroom researching to boardroom briefings took a lot of effort, planning, and a solid foundational understanding of how to conduct threat hunts.

On this particular occasion, Cyber Sleuths International was contacted by a privately owned organization employing around 10,000 individuals. Over the past 12 months, they had been having an increasing array of *issues* cropping up throughout their business. It all started after the previous year's *leadership summit*, during which all of the department leads traveled to a resort for a week to plan out the upcoming year's goals and objectives. One of the members on the retreat brought back an adware virus that propagated a portion of the company network, resulting in extensive overtime for the system administrators over the course of a few weeks. A month or two later, the company had its first major blow when a product that was in the late stages of development was released by a competitor with almost identical specifications. Following that devastating event, the company began experiencing an increasing slowdown in its production cycle. More and more systems were experiencing technical glitches requiring third-party engineers to be brought on site to re-baseline the operational environment. The final straw for the organization was when one of those engineers identified a software library on one of the production machines that was *different* from the standard deployment.

While the initial discussion was very brief, it was clear to Cyber Sleuths International that this organization was experiencing a concentration of catastrophes that was impacting their long-term financial stability. What first appeared as some bad luck within the company slowly simmered into the concern of cyber espionage. Cyber Sleuths International was hired to conduct a comprehensive hunt for any adversary that might be present on the network that was causing these events. Reluctantly, the CEO agreed to the expenditure of contracting the threat hunters on a limited basis. They were allowed to work on site with a system administrator and the security team only as long as it didn't impact operations. Additionally, this case had to be wrapped up within the next month as anything past that could further impact the organization's production capability during their busy season.

During Cyber Sleuths' introduction into the organization, they set a few hours aside to discuss the wants and needs of the organization with the organization's stakeholders and technical experts. During this time, they completed the NIST CSF in order to gain a better grasp of where the organization perceived themselves, their priorities, and gaps in the defense. From there, they discussed the type and scope of the proposed threat hunt to be conducted. After some in-depth discussions, it was identified that the hunt would be based on a high intelligence/low network knowledge construct. While there were plenty of indications into the threat actor that was suspected, the organization had done an overall slow job of baselining the network. This caused all members to have an overall poor understanding of what to expect and what should be considered *normal* network activity.

The following is a high-level version of a completed CSF crafted during this onboarding. This is one method of completion that could be utilized by the threat hunting team in order to gain a better understanding of the landscape. A more complete write-up can also be found in the *Appendix*:

Functions	Categories	Sub-categories	Response
Identify			
	Asset Management	Inventory of software systems	We inventory all software on company devices. We do allow BYOD, but that's usually just for email.
	Asset Management	Inventory of hardware (online)	Again, we inventory all on-premises devices. There are some remote workers we'll ask for their serial numbers. BYOD we don't because those are personal items.

The previous sampling of foundational activities will provide insight into the *who* and *what* of the business. A full listing will include details on the business environment and risk management strategy. This leads to the requirement outlining the existing safeguards for those items.

Functions	Categories	Sub-categories	Response
Protect			
	Identification management	Remote access is managed	Remote users have to log in with their normal credentials to the VPN device.
	Awareness training	All users are informed and trained	Users are trained on our processes and requirements when they're hired. We've had some employees for 20 years!
	Protective technology	Audit/log records are determined, documented, and reviewed	We keep 30 days of logs as long as the storage allows it. We're looking to upgrade our log servers from 2015.

A full listing of the **protect** function will include all identity management and access controls, training, maintenance, and security technologies in place. These items will allow the organization to better comprehend the capabilities that exist to detect any cybersecurity events that occur.

Functions	Categories	Sub-categories	Response
Detect			
	Anomalies and events	A baseline of network operations is accomplished	We baseline the network every Sunday night, or after a major upgrade to IT.
	Security continuous monitoring	The network is monitored to detect events	We have the IT individuals look at any alarms that come into the email inbox.
		Vulnerability scans performed	We vulnerability scan the IT and workforce desktops; some of the servers we can't scan because it would break them.

An expanded **detection** function will include additional sections, including anomalies and events, continuous monitoring, and the full detection process. These items will lead to the organization's capability to respond to those items detected.

Functions	Categories	Sub-categories	Response
Respond			
	Communications	Personnel know their role and order of ops	IT knows to call the executives when something goes wrong
	Mitigation	New vulnerabilities are mitigated or risks accepted	New vulnerabilities are discovered by watching the news and we discuss what risks there are before accepting them.

A comprehensive **respond** function will map out additional areas, such as planning for those responses, communications, and mitigations. With a fully articulated response function, the organization will be able to move on to the final function.

Functions	Categories	Sub-categories	Response
Recover			
	Communications	Reputation is repaired after an incident	We only notify customers if there's data loss; that's all that's required as per our law firm
	Improvements	Recovery incorporates lessons learned	We give the report to IT and let them do what needs to be fixed within their budget.

The **recovery** function will include recovery planning, improvements required, and follow-on communication strategies. A full listing of these items can be found in the *NIST Framework for Improving Critical Infrastructure Cybersecurity*.

Summary

Understanding an organization's requirements and underlying motivations will be critical in conducting a successful threat hunt. Each organization will have its own business priorities, concerns, and regulatory and legal requirements. A team must firmly grasp these before progressing down the path of conducting a threat hunt. One such way to do this is to utilize the CSF developed by NIST. This is a great framework that allows anyone from a small team to an entire organization to outline their needs and priorities.

Use the organization's goals and needs to make sure resources are being applied in the areas that matter the most. Understand and communicate with stakeholders what type of threat hunt you want to conduct and what the organizational environment is capable of supporting. With the overview of addressing and scoping hunts to business needs and requirements completed, the next area for focus is how the team is constructed. In the next chapter, we will look at the individual roles and the responsibilities each team member will need to fill.

Review questions

Answer the following questions to check your knowledge of this chapter:

1. (Fill in the blanks) A _____ is a requirement that is established outside of the control of the organization. A _____ is a requirement that is established within the control of an organization. _____ are neither of these; however, they are considered good things to consider.

2. Which of the following are organizational-level benefits to conducting a threat hunt?

    A. Validation of threat intelligence reporting in relation to the organization being targeted

    B. Re-enforces stakeholders' trust in the confidentiality, integrity, and availability of the network

    C. Increases the understanding of the enterprise and how systems interact

3. If the organization wants a hunt team that does not have any bias, and cost is a major influence, should they attempt to establish an internal team or hire an external team?

4. What are the five main requirements for a successful threat hunt?

Review answers

The answers to the review questions are as follows:

1. Regulation, policies, best practices. See the *Regulatory requirements, legalities, and best practices* section for more information.

2. A, B. At a high level, an organization does concern itself with the standard traffic patterns and behaviors of users. Those items are extremely beneficial to defenders and administrators when identifying that something is wrong.

3. External team. While an external team has higher short-term costs, an internal team will cost more to maintain and will normally come with organizational bias.

4. An organization that wants to have a threat hunt conducted; an organization that is willing and capable of granting the necessary access and authority for the threat hunting team; an organization that is willing and capable of integrating the results of the threat hunt into their defenses and business processes; a threat hunting team with the appropriate processes, training, and equipment; a plan that satisfies business requirements and identifies a goal for the team to attempt to achieve.

3
Team Construct

When constructing the line-up of a team, the goal is normally to have an effective hunt team that can tackle a specific objective with very little flailing. A team's construct will be unique in each organization and situation. Just as no two threat hunts are exactly the same, no two teams will be exactly the same. They will, however, have some shared fundamental concepts.

Assembling a highly effective hunt team takes time for both the organization and the individuals concerned. Certifications, degrees, and experience are all nice to have; however, they will all mean very little if the people behind them do not have the proper drive or mindset. Always start with personnel that is driven to unravel the puzzles they find in cybersecurity, and go from there. You can build people up into the positions that are needed if they have the proper mindset.

In this chapter, we are going to cover the following topics:

- Roles performed within a team
- Training requirements
- Ways to organize a team
- Scenario A – internal threat hunt
- Scenario B – external threat hunt

By the end of the chapter, you will be able to do the following:

- *Discuss* the main roles required within an effective hunt team.
- *Comprehend* the expectations each individual role will need to fulfill.
- *Identify* different considerations when building a team to meet an organizational need.

Roles performed within a team

Regardless of a team's size or purpose, each team will have certain roles that must be fulfilled by the members. If the word *roles* sounds too strict, then let's call them *functions* instead. Whatever they are called, the ones listed within this book are generic in nature and should be molded as necessary to fit the needs of the team.

The first question that is normally asked by an employer who is managing the resources is this: *Do you really need all of those people?* The number of resources provided to the team is something that can be debated and can fluctuate with activity. The roles needed are the same if there are 2 or 10 people on the team.

Seven roles will be required throughout the course of the threat hunt, as listed here:

- Team lead
- Host-based analyst
- Network-based analyst
- **Threat intelligence** (**TI**) analyst
- Incident responder/security analyst
- Network administrator
- Client system/server administrator

The first three roles must be performed by personnel directly assigned to the team and cannot be outsourced to a non-dedicated team member or individual within the organization. When positions are outsourced outside of permanently assigned team members, this mixture of personnel is sometimes referred to as a hybrid team. The last four roles can either be performed by personnel dedicated to the team or by personnel outside of the team, the main difference being that those resources belonging to a team can be controlled and directed by the team. Resources belonging to another entity cannot be directly controlled and might have different priorities.

When building out a team, remember that nothing can replace face-to-face interaction with a customer. At times, it is worthwhile having fewer analysts on a hunt conducted at a customer's location than to have extra personnel virtually and miss that physical interaction.

The following work roles include an overview for each position, as well as general responsibilities for each. A much more detailed framework can be found in the **National Institute for Standards and Technology (NIST)** work roles document, located here: `https://niccs.cisa.gov/workforce-development/cyber-security-workforce-framework/workroles`.

Team lead

NIST work role: Cyber Operations (Ops) Planner

This role will lead the team both from an internal and external standpoint. Whoever fulfills this role is the *face* of the team and is responsible for all interactions with the customer. Another way to look at it is that they are the ones who will be standing before the customer, explaining what happened and whether it was good or bad.

A leader guides people; a manager guides processes. Keep this in mind while contemplating the *team lead* role.

Due to the immensity of this function, it is best to have a dedicated team lead who does not have a critical secondary position. While a team lead can find time to conduct analysis or research, their primary purpose during the hunt is facilitation. The first challenge that they will face is being the go-between for customers and analysts while ensuring that the analysts stay within the lanes of what is required and has been explicitly allowed by the customers.

In order for them to be an effective filter between customers and analysts, the team lead must be highly skilled in all forms of communication. If a prospective team lead feels that communication is mainly about what is said or typed in an email, then they are not the one for this role. Simple things such as misspelled words, poor regional/social etiquette, or even improper physical communication can stop a threat hunt before it even gets off the ground. All these communication quirks will impact how requirements are communicated, interpreted, and then responded to by another entity. To put it plainly, words matter, so the team lead will need to be well versed in communicating with a purpose.

When it comes to the title of *team lead*, the concept of leading people will need to be the main focus. In doing so, the team lead will need to be capable and willing to receive feedback from the team and take action on this new information. While doing so, communication will remain key and should never stop between all entities. If a team member attempts to provide feedback but the lead never provides follow-up in return, the team member will be left to their own assumptions on what happened and could end up feeling ignored. *Lead* is in the title, and taking care of people is what a leader does.

With all of the focus on communication and people, there is still a threat hunt to perform. The team lead must be able to help guide the hunt while managing conflicting timelines, priorities, and requests for resources. Plans change and will need to be adjusted as the threat hunt progresses, and decisions will have to be made about which target to look into. A team lead must be able to receive feedback from the team, align it with the customer requirements and limitations, and provide a way forward for all to follow.

Of all of the positions on the team, this is the only one that does not *have* to be technical in nature. With that in mind, I have only seen it work that way successfully in a handful of instances. If the lead is not highly technical, then they must be highly knowledgeable in all other areas of the mission and have already established themselves as a strong leader within the team. If nothing else is understood about this position, know that this person must be a leader of people and not just a manager of processes.

A summary of a team lead's responsibilities is the following:

- Ensuring effective communication within the team
- Ensuring effective communication with the customer
- Ensuring required deliverables are achieved and provided to the customer
- Managing personnel and equipment safety
- Establishing and adhering to rules of engagement, authorizations, and communication contracts
- Ensuring successful execution of the hunt

Host-based analyst

NIST work role: Cyber Defense Analyst

The host-based analyst role is a highly technical position that focuses on all things that occur on workstations and servers. When aligning this role with the **Open Systems Interconnection** (**OSI**) model, a host-based analyst would focus on the top three layers. The first misconception that occurs with this role is thinking that a host-based analyst and a forensic analyst are the same thing. They're similar in the same way that a bicycle and a motorcycle are similar. While a forensic analyst will be able to conduct reverse engineering of complex programs and worries about things such as the chain of customers, a host-based analyst will only go slightly below the surface in order to conduct analysis.

Examples of typical activities that a host-based analyst can be expected to perform are correlating and analyzing host logs, high-level language static file review, and basic memory analysis. If during the course of their activities something is believed to be malicious but cannot be readily identified, then a specialist—sometimes referred to as a Tier-3 forensic analyst—can be called upon to assist.

This role can be combined with the upcoming network-based analyst role, which is one of the first big decisions the team lead will need to make. Combining the two roles puts the analyst in a position where they will have a wider scope of data to review but can hopefully see an entire picture of what is happening. Keeping the roles separate can reduce the insight the host- or network-based analyst has but would allow them to focus heavily on their specific role and potentially identify evidence that would have been overlooked otherwise.

There is no explicit right or wrong way to structure these roles—it is solely dependent upon the scope of the hunt and the number of resources available. If hunting across a large enterprise with a small team is a priority, combining the roles would be beneficial to allow the review of all data points. If hunting for an increased number of indicators or hypotheses is the priority, then keeping them separate can prove to be beneficial. Time is also a factor to consider when determining how to align the role resources. If time is short, more people filling dedicated roles can move through information faster.

Whichever method is chosen, the host-based analyst will have one final requirement levied on them: they will need to be highly effective at both verbal and written communication. This does not play as much a part during the initial stand-up of the threat hunt as it does during and after the execution. If a host-based analyst found something malicious on a workstation and stated so in the team's mission log that records significant events that occurred, will the other roles be able to understand what is going on? An analyst that is well versed in communication will be able to effectively articulate what happened, where it happened, any **identifiers** (**IDs**), requested actions, and follow-up requirements, to list a few items.

A summary of a host-based analyst's responsibilities includes the following:

- Conducting host-level analysis

- Researching common and recently identified **indicators of compromise (IoCs)**

- Scripting design and implementation in order to automate detection and management activities

- Possessing basic-level knowledge of Windows, macOS, and Linux/Unix

- Understanding of the team's toolsets utilized to acquire, analyze, and enrich host data

- Understanding of key system files and locations, baseline configurations, normal processes and their behaviors, memory management, artifact locations, methods of system interaction, and how they behave at the system level

- Conducting basic forensic analysis on files using tools such as a hex editor

- Conducting basic forensic analysis on memory dumps

- Providing feedback to leadership on the status of the hunt

- Communicating with the entire team on events as they are discovered

Network-based analyst

NIST work role: Cyber Defense Analyst

The network-based analyst role is another highly technical position that focuses on all activities that occur across the network. When aligning this role with the OSI model, a network-based analyst would focus on the bottom four layers. As mentioned in the previous section, this role can be combined with a host-based analyst's role to make a generic analyst role. The pros and cons of combining will change depending upon the requirements, constraints, and restraints of the threat hunt. Ensure that you critically analyze and identify the impacts before deciding what to do with the analyst roles.

The only other area of note to be mindful of when identifying a network-based analyst requirement is whether the target network will be **information technology (IT)**-based or **operational technology (OT)**-based. If this is the first time the team is contemplating the difference between the two, stay away from any and all OT networks. Teams that threat hunt on an OT network should have additional training and a deeper understanding of the technologies employed, along with the different constraints that will be levied upon them.

Just as with the previous two roles, network-based analysts will need to be highly effective at both verbal and written communication. If a network-based analyst found something malicious traversing the network and stated so in a mission log, will the other analyst be able to understand what is going on? An analyst that is well versed in communication will be able to effectively articulate what happened, where it happened, any IDs, requested actions, and follow-up requirements.

A summary of a network-based analyst's responsibilities includes the following:

- Conducting network-level analysis
- Researching common and recent network attack indicators
- Constructing scripts to automate activities
- Possessing basic-level knowledge of networking protocols and encryption standards
- Understanding of the team's toolsets utilized to acquire, analyze, and enrich network data
- Understanding expected protocol behaviors and standards
- Providing feedback to leadership on the status of the hunt
- Communicating with the entire team on events as they are discovered

TI analyst

NIST work role: All-Source Analyst

A TI analyst is one of those roles that, if you conduct threat hunting long enough, you will have to justify to leadership or a customer as to why they matter.

Without intelligence, can you conduct a threat hunt? Yes

Will that threat hunt be successful at catching a skillful adversary? Chances are no unless that adversary is being blatantly *loud*, in which case, you will find them but most likely without understanding their intentions. (See *Lockheed Martin Cyber Kill Chain* in *Chapter 4, Communication Breakdown*, for a deeper dive on why this matters.)

What does a TI analyst provide? They provide meaning to the indicators that are being hunted. They give context to the data that is being analyzed. Analysts can identify traffic patterns and events that occur, and a TI analyst will help link them together to identify larger threat-actor **tactics, techniques, and procedures** (**TTPs**). If enough information is able to be placed together, assumptions can begin to form, and a perception of an adversary's intentions might begin to arise.

With the reasons for needing a TI analyst out of the way, what do they provide? TI analysts will provide targeting information for other analysts to look for and enrichment of evidence that has been identified. The manner and speed at which this occurs will be based upon the organization and the experience level of the analyst.

A very rudimentary real-world example would be if an individual were told to go outside and *hunt* for rocks. An intelligence analyst would inform them that rocks of interest tend to all be yellow in tone. The rock hunter would come back with an armful of rocks. The intelligence analyst could then review the pile and tell them which ones were actually pyrite and which ones were real gold, along with why you most likely found them in the company parking lot.

It is worth repeating that all analysts must be highly effective at both written and verbal communication. Without effective communication, the entire process will dry up and become ineffective.

A summary of a TI analyst's responsibilities includes the following:

- Providing targeted threat indicators to other analysts
- Reviewing and enriching investigation evidence
- Researching public, private, and dark web repositories for additional indicators or significant correlation activity
- Ensuring community TI is appropriately vetted, integrated, and able to be consumed by the appropriate systems/analysts
- Reporting on specific threats or targets to members within and outside of the threat-hunting team
- Providing feedback to leadership on the status of the hunt
- Communicating with the entire team on events as they occur

Incident responder/security analyst

NIST work role: Cyber Defense Incident Responder

An incident responder will normally have two overarching questions in mind when they conduct investigations: *What is the root cause of the malicious activity and what is the scope of that activity?* These questions can be asked of hunt analysts to provide an answer to the organization. Doing so is not the worst thing, and it can provide greater flexibility to the analyst in certain situations. Just remember that while the hunt analyst is investigating to identify the root cause and scope, they are not hunting for other indicators.

Once those two questions are answered, an incident responder will also be involved in the remediation of the event, whereas a hunt analyst is not. As such, it is extremely beneficial to have personnel involved in the remediation that was a part of the incident response to ensure an adequate understanding of the situation. For this reason, it should be the default setup to have a separate role filled by an incident responder and not utilize a hunt analyst to attempt to answer the root cause-and-scope questions.

Scenario: A threat hunt is trying to find evidence of a specific threat actor. Here are two possible ways this could be dealt with:

- **Scenario 1**: An analyst acting as both a hunter and incident responder found evidence of that specific threat actor—mission success. Having the latitude to finish the investigation is advantageous as they already have the knowledge in place. Doing so is not a detriment to the overarching objective of the hunt.

- **Scenario 2**: A team with a separate analyst and incident responder is conducting a similar hunt. That particular hunt analyst found evidence of a different threat actor. Being able to hand that off to an incident responder will allow the hunt analyst to continue striving to reach their objective while allowing the organization to track down and remediate the parallel threat.

Once again, communication is paramount, in that all members of the team must be able to effectively communicate both verbally and in writing.

A summary of an incident responder's/security analyst's responsibilities includes the following:

- Investigating any detected event that meets an established threshold to identify the root cause and scope of activity

- Participating in the organization's remediation process as needed

- Providing feedback to leadership on the status of any events connected to the hunt

Network administrator

NIST work role: Network Operations Specialist

Simply put, this role is responsible for ensuring all infrastructure and equipment utilized by the hunt team is in working order throughout the mission. While this can be outsourced to a non-team member, the team will be at the mercy of the priority of the owning entity when something breaks. No one will care about a broken piece of equipment nearly as much as the people trying to use it.

The other potential restraint for this role is whether it should be combined with another role. The default answer should be *no* as an analyst and administrator have conflicting priorities. However, there are instances where this must occur due to constraints placed upon the team. If a team of two individuals is sent to a remote location to conduct a threat hunt, there will not be latitude to have both a dedicated analyst and a dedicated administrator.

A summary of a network administrator's responsibilities includes the following:

- Maintaining all infrastructure utilized by the hunt team to include infrastructure deployed throughout the target network
- Can be combined with client system/server administrator

Client system/server administrator

NIST work role: System Administrator

This role is focused on the existing administrators of the target network. While this is not normally a dedicated member of the team, do not overlook the value that this role provides. Having personnel that can answer questions and explain the purpose behind certain behaviors or traffic is absolutely invaluable. Include these members as a part of the team from the beginning, keep the lines of communication open, and the team will have a much lower chance of spending the entire hunt chasing after a bad management configuration.

A summary of a client/system server administrator's responsibilities includes the following:

- Maintaining all systems and software utilized by the hunt team to include sensors deployed throughout the target network
- Can be combined with a network administrator role if the threat-hunt team is part of the same organization as the target hunt

The seven roles listed previously are the main *types* of positions and functions performed by a hunt team. This is by no means a definitive list that must be adhered to. If a team's hunt has a unique requirement, then the team leadership should not hesitate to adjust the line-up to fit the requirements. Some instances, such as hunting on an OT network, could require the addition of a few different **subject-matter experts** (**SMEs**) who do nothing more than guide the team. Always tailor the team to meet the requirements of each engagement; never work the other way around.

Training requirements

It can be very hard to narrow down what sort of training is the *correct* training for any team or individual. There are always new technologies, threats, and vulnerabilities each and every day. One place that can help a newer team is to start building a baseline of what could be required from each position within your team based upon *NIST Special Publication 800-181 Revision 1* (`https://nvlpubs.nist.gov/nistpubs/ SpecialPublications/NIST.SP.800-181r1.pdf`).

This framework has all of the standard roles broken out by function that you can then look closer at. Each will have a breakout of typical skills and knowledge functions that are required to perform the tasks expected of those roles. Take time to design and document the capabilities you want in a hunt team. Once you have your *baseline* established, start building—or hiring—people toward those goals, then grow them beyond that.

The following link provides an easy-to-use search function to identify your needed work role and associated abilities, knowledge, skills, and tasks for that position: `https:// niccs.cisa.gov/workforce-development/cyber-security-workforce- framework/workroles#`.

Ways to organize a team

As with many things in threat hunting, a team's organization will be dependent upon many different factors. Some organizations have a rigid structure mandated from the top down on how *project teams* will be organized. Some might have certain requirements and priorities that give extra flexibility when forming a team. Regardless of whether a team is coming in as a third party or organic to an organization, certain criteria must be taken into account.

When organizing a team, keep in mind that you can combine roles and responsibilities. If you decide to combine functions, walk through the impacts that the decision will have and ensure it is something that the team can work with.

For example, we can look at what would happen if we had a single team member acting as both a host-based analyst and a server administrator. This would result in an individual that is expected to both utilize and maintain the tools that the team employs. When a part of the hunt toolkit inevitably breaks, then the team will be down an analyst until the system is operational again. A member can't be in two places at once, resulting in the team being partially capable as one of the analysts is no longer reviewing data and is instead performing maintenance on the team's systems.

In a complementary example, a team member acting as a host-based analyst and a network-based analyst provides an analyst that can hunt both on host systems and through network data. Training requirements would be increased as the target domains are completely different. However, a single analyst could perform hunt activities for either without stopping, as the priorities for both are the same. However, again, a team member can't do both at the same time.

The way a team should be organized will be based upon the following criteria:

- **Resources available (personnel, monetary, equipment)**: Sometimes, hunting is not a priority that an organization is willing to dedicate resources toward. This is part of the back-and-forth adjustment. Increase the available resources, and things could be done a degree faster or with a larger scope. Decrease the available resources, and the time to completion increases or the scope of the hunt decreases. Sometimes, the resource availability isn't an organizational restraint but, rather, a constraint by an outside entity. Some countries do not allow ingress or egress of certain technologies, which will ultimately limit the type and amount of equipment the hunt team brings.

- **Time (operating threat hunt 24/7 or only during normal business hours)**: Time scarcity is a fairly straightforward conundrum for any organization. A team might want to work in shifts split up throughout a 24-hour cycle in order to get more work done. However, doing so takes up more resources and could require the cooperation of the requesting customer, as not all organizations work throughout the night. Additionally, if the threat-hunt team is attempting to blend in and not be obvious on the network, then sticking to normal business hours would be suggested.

- **Scope of network/hunt versus time the organization is allowing**: This is the other piece opposite to resource availability that flexes on a non-linear scale. If an organization wants a team to hunt on a network with a million nodes and complete it in under a month, the team size will drastically increase. If the time increases, the scope and team size will need to shift accordingly.

- **Type of network (IT versus OT versus cloud)**: An IT network is what the vast majority of personnel are experienced with. OT networks are very similar in nature but have a lot of different protocols and equipment on the network. Additionally, the priorities for what matters tend to be night and day between IT and OT. Cloud networks are the same in the sense that the ways you would want to acquire data, analyze, and possibly identify the root cause of events would each be different. Selecting the right individuals can be critical for the hunt to be successful.

- **Data accessible (only able to acquire new passive traffic versus analysis of live and historical host and network data):** During initial discussions with the customer, the acquisition of data will be outlined. Which parts of the network will the team have access to? What type of data will be approved to be captured, and how will this be done? Are there any historical references for the same dataset available? Expectation management is key. In the past, organizations have expected teams to sign off that they had conducted a threat hunt on their network but only wanted to grant them access to the **demilitarized zone (DMZ)**.

- **Multiple hunt locations/multiple team locations (on-site and a remote team):** Sometimes, a single location or network just isn't enough. If the target location for the threat hunt is costly, sending data back to a more accessible location for the rest of the team might be beneficial. The biggest challenge in this area is having the owning organization agree to the data leaving their networks.

These questions then start to bleed into other topics already discussed in this chapter, such as the following: *Will the team have a dedicated host- and network-based analyst or will there be a combined hunt analyst? Also, who will maintain the equipment—a dedicated technician, or will an analyst be shouldering that responsibility?* We will now pick up with our scenarios to see how the new information covered in this chapter will be incorporated.

Scenario A – internal threat hunt

After an initial discussion with the **chief executive officer (CEO)** of *Widget Makers Inc.*, the team lead was able to select a five-member on-site team that would be able to best operate within the constraints provided while still achieving the organization's goals. The teams agreed upon a list of deliverables for their inaugural threat hunt, as follows:

- Initial team roster and itemized equipment required for the establishment of the internal team

- Real-time feedback on any identified threats during the course of the threat hunt

- Leadership and technical debrief, along with a written report of the threat hunt, each objective, and recommendations for follow-on actions

- Technical debrief and report of the threat hunt for system administrators, to include specific actions taken and recommendations for follow-on activity

The internal hunt team will consist of the following:

- **1x team lead**: This individual will not only be leading the hunt, but they will also be ensuring that the team will continue to grow beyond their initial founding construct. Prior to each hunt, the team lead will be responsible for ensuring that the team has all the needed training, materials, and resources to successfully attempt the mission before them. After each hunt, this individual will be responsible for ensuring all deliverables are provided to the applicable stakeholders and that the team completes its reconstitution phase to be ready for the next event.

- **2x analysts (host-based and network-based)**: Due to the smaller team size, these analysts will be responsible for reviewing data originating both on host systems and network devices. Between them, they will provide feedback to the team lead on any additional data that should be collected and retained.

- **1x network administrator**: This team opted to have a dedicated network administrator on the team. While this will take away a position that could be utilized for analyzing data, it will allow someone to focus on the maintenance of the team's equipment. The benefit is that if something breaks, a *trusted member* of the team will be able to recover it without impacting the team's throughput capability or asking a third party for assistance.

- **1x TI analyst**: During the team's first threat hunt, expectations for the TI analyst will be lower than that of a more established team. The TI analyst will have two main purposes: expand upon the **Federal Bureau of Investigation (FBI)**-provided **open source intelligence (OSINT)** briefing as it is related to *Widget Makers Inc.*, and provide additional context for any data points of interest that are discovered by the hunt team. After each mission, the TI analyst will be expected to continue to grow the organization's understanding of itself and how others perceive it within the broader cyber landscape.

With the team positions identified, the correct individuals must be identified and any shortfalls such as training should begin immediately.

Scenario B – external threat hunt

After a review of the constraints, restraints, and scope of the network, *Cyber Sleuths International* determined that a five-member on-site team would work best to meet the organization's needs. The customer has agreed to provide additional support in the form of a system administrator, which will turn the hunt team into a hybrid model. Doing so will allow the team a higher level of insight into how the enterprise has been developed and managed. A list of the team's agreed-upon deliverables to provide to the organization is provided here:

- Targeted organizational threat briefing. This will consist of open source research concerning who is *targeting* their organization or organizations like them, and those actors' known offensive cyber capabilities, motivating factors, and best practices for defense.

- Real-time feedback on any identified threats during the course of the threat hunt.

- Leadership debrief and report of the threat hunt, each objective, and recommendations for follow-on actions.

- Technical debrief and report of the threat hunt for system administrators, to include specific actions taken and recommendations for follow-on activity.

The *Cyber Sleuths International* threat-hunt team will consist of the following:

- **1x team lead**: This individual will be responsible for identifying requirements, leading planning, and ensuring the team stays within its authorized areas and achieves its objectives. The vast majority of communication with the organizational leadership will be through the team lead. *Cyber Sleuths International* has found that this is the easiest way to provide a single communication channel to the organization while minimizing misunderstandings from the team.

- **1x host-based analyst and 1x network-based analyst**: The primary host-based and primary network-based analysts are responsible for ensuring that their target set is successfully collected and retained. Any new data retrieval or capture will fall within the scope and responsibilities of these individuals.

- **1x security analyst/network administrator**: This security analyst will also perform the network administrator role for the team. They will establish and maintain the base of operations that the team will utilize for the duration of the mission. Post mission, they will be responsible for the destruction of any data that is not authorized to leave the organization's network.

- **1x TI analyst**: This TI analyst will act as a primary research and correlation capability for any data of interest that is retrieved throughout the course of the mission. The organization requested that a targeted intelligence briefing also be provided by *Cyber Sleuths International*. This analyst will develop this deliverable prior to the start of the event.

- **1x system administrator**: This administrator will act as primary contact for integrating any new sensors throughout the enterprise or retrieving new datasets from systems. During the length of the hunt mission, their primary responsibility will be to aid and support the hunt team.

With the team positions identified, the correct individuals must be identified and any shortfalls such as training should begin immediately.

Summary

Regardless of the number of personnel on a team, certain roles must be fulfilled. Communication will play a critical role at all stages of the threat hunt and from all members of the team. This process will be overseen by the team lead position. Whether there are 2 individuals or 25, there will always be a team lead.

Host- and network-based analyst roles are a little more flexible and can be combined if it is the right fit for the hunt. Additionally, a TI analyst will always be a major boost for a hunt team, so fight for them to be included. **Incident response** (**IR**) personnel are a part of an organization's remediation process—threat-hunt analysts are not. When in doubt, leverage *NIST Special Publication 800-181 Revision 1, Workforce Framework for Cybersecurity (NICE Framework)*, to build out the hunt team's capability requirements and training pathways.

There is no one correct way to build a team—each hunt will be unique, and the team should be tailored to its particular requirements. Now that the design of the team is coming into focus, we will move on to the one factor that will make or break any organization, team, or partnership: *communication*, which we will discuss in the next chapter. This is where the vast majority of hunts ultimately break down and failures begin to occur, as communication is something that must be continually accomplished.

Review questions

Answer the following questions to check your knowledge of this chapter:

1. Which of the following functions must be fulfilled on a hunt team?

    A. Team lead

    B. Host-/network-based analyst

    C. TI analyst

    D. Network administrator

2. Which role is responsible for all internal and external communication conducted by a hunt team?

3. Which role is normally not a dedicated member of the hunt team yet still participates in their mission?

4. Who is responsible for effective communication within the team as well as providing feedback to leadership on how the hunt is progressing?

5. Name at least two of the six considerations when building out a hunt team.

Review answers

The answers to the review questions are as follows:

1. A, B
2. Team lead
3. Client system/server administrator
4. All team members
5. Resources available, time available, the scope of the hunt, type of network, data accessible during the hunt, location of the hunt

4
Communication Breakdown

Whatever the activity, anything that involves more than a single entity will require communication in some form. Without successful communication, that activity will fail. Communication is the glue that holds individuals and actions together as a single unit. The communication required during threat hunting is no different in this aspect.

To start things out, let's outline the four distinct ways in which individuals can communicate:

- **Visual**: This method of communication takes the form of information that can be seen, such as a video showing how to complete a specific task or a picture in a report providing insight into a behavior.

- **Written**: This includes all aspects of communication through the use of written words. This book is an example of written communication.

- **Verbal**: This is a method of vocalizing information. Volume, tone, and inflections all play a major part in how this method is perceived.

- **Non-verbal**: This is all of the behavioral-based methods of communication. Body posture, eye contact, hand movements, and even the way we are dressed are all examples.

The preceding methods are ways in which an individual can send a message, but there are a lot more factors to consider for the entire communication process. Some of those items are as follows:

- **Environment**: Verbal communication in a noisy room will impede proper reception of the information.

- **Method of delivery**: Messy handwriting on a crumpled piece of paper will covey a different message than clean and precise writing in a professional report.

- **Bias**: Personal bias and preconceived notions will obscure a receiving party's expectations prior to a message being sent. Many times, this can carry a heavier impact than the actual words used by the sender.

- **Cultural diversity**: Different cultures have different expectations; an unintended blunder or slip-up could change the recipient's view more than the actual message itself.

When communicating, take the time and try to know your audience. If you are working in a new organization or country, do your research ahead of time and identify any expectations or social etiquette to be mindful of. If you are delivering an introductory briefing to a senior leader that does not have a technical background, then do not present them with any technical jargon or data. Some cultures are very mindful of the way they are perceived; correcting people openly in a room full of others could get you barred from any future contact.

These communication rules are not just for the team lead; they extend to anyone that will interact with the customer. If the team is working with an outside organization, understand that first impressions mean everything. People will tend to default to the idea of whoever is dressed the nicest is probably in charge. Set the grooming and dress standards for the team and ensure everyone is presenting the image that they intend to present.

In this chapter, we are going to cover the following topics:

- Internal team communication
- Communicating with stakeholders
- Communicating with other administrators
- Communicating with the adversary
- Positive and negative non-verbal languages
- Scenario A—internal threat hunt
- Scenario B—external threat hunt

By the end of the chapter, you will be able to do the following:

- *Identify* the different participants within a hunt that the team will communicate with.
- *Comprehend* the different considerations that should be taken when communicating with each group of participants.
- *Discuss* the different non-verbal methods of communication that can occur.

Internal team communication

Internal team communication tends to be the easiest, by far, for people to understand the requirements for and adhere to. The first step is to identify communication needs for the team, such as applications that provide day-to-day continuity, have the ability to store files, and have encrypted communication with authentication. No team wants to be in the position where their hunt failed due to an adversary monitoring the hunt team's communication in real time.

Chat programs such as Slack, Microsoft Teams, and Rocket.Chat work well for day-to-day communications. If someone stepped out for a moment or if you have teams spread out and working remotely, even if it's within one customer complex, everyone can remain on the same page on the most up-to-date status of the hunt. Additionally, chat programs provide an amazing source of historical context for things that happened earlier in a shift or even the previous week.

> **Important Note**
> If anything of importance is communicated to the team verbally, always follow up with the same message in a written medium. A team chat program works well for this or even through an email. This will help ensure delivery to all members, as well as reducing the likelihood of someone "hearing" the wrong message.

At a minimum, the team needs to establish individual chat channels for the following areas:

- **Operator channel**: Only operators should talk here. Communication will be very fast and loose with a high degree of freedom to vocalize theories and hypotheses. This will be the *Wild West* of communication areas. Highly discourage allowing a customer or senior leadership into operator channels in all but the most extreme circumstances.

- **C2 channel**: Can be combined with the *Operator channel* if a single team is conducting the threat hunt. All members will need to monitor this channel as it will be the primary method for the team lead to conduct and document **command and control** (**C2**) activities. This channel should be limited to only team members without the customer in order to allow free flow of communication within the team and control the line of communication with the customer.

- **Intel channel**: All members should monitor this periodically as this is the primary location for intel to receive **requests for information** (**RFIs**) and respond to inquiries.

- **Customer channel**: Select team members and customers can have membership here in order to interact and communicate with one another if they are not co-located.

There are also other tools, such as wiki applications and programs such as Jupyter Notebooks, that work great for highly detailed **tactic, technique, and procedure** (**TTP**) coordination. Whatever the solution that is chosen, the team lead should instill the standard that all operators must utilize a notepad or some local-to-their-endpoint application to keep "operator notes." These notes should contain all commands that have been run, their results, the context for why they were used, the mindset/methodology employed by the operator, and so on. This aids massively in preventing operator error as well as ensuring each member can provide meaningful feedback during each day's debrief.

> **Real-World Example**
>
> During one threat hunting mission, analysts were instructed to never type directly into a command prompt. Any action interacting directly with a target system was to be written out by the member in their operator notes and reviewed by a second analyst before executing. One team member ceased adhering to this requirement halfway through their shift and began typing directly into a domain controller's command prompt. Before long, they tried to clean up their own log files and almost formatted the entire system. Thankfully, tertiary safety protocols were in place that prevented those systems from being deleted. Never interact directly with a target system unless you know exactly what you are typing and why and it has been validated by another member that it is correct.

Communicating with stakeholders

Once your attempted communications are created and leave your control, they are now out there for others to interpret and act on. The first rule of interacting with a customer is to state only facts. Do not attempt to change the appearance of a situation or finding to be better or worse than it is. If you do not know why something happened, do not pretend you do. Unless you saw a person at a keyboard performing malicious activities, then you do not know who was performing those actions even if it was their account. Threat hunters and red teams have caused personnel to lose jobs over misrepresentation and poor communication of facts. Stick to the facts.

When it inevitably happens that someone asks for an opinion, minimize the response if it cannot be avoided altogether. A hunt team is there to give the facts not to state someone's motives or whether it was a specific individual that performed an action. Anytime an opinion or assumption is communicated, ensure that it is explicitly framed as such.

> Example
> "The account in question exhibited this type of malicious behavior, which led the team to perceive the user's intentions of obtaining access to this other system. This is an assumption as the individual executing these activities does not appear to have completed their actions at this time."

Communicating with other administrators

The day-to-day organizational defenders, administrators, and users will be operating on the network at the same time as the threat hunting team. Ensuring open communications will be crucial in order to prevent duplication of effort or friendly fire against legitimate users or systems. Include these other members as part of the team from day 1. If possible, allow them access to the same communication channels as the team. If the hunt team and administrators are located in the same area, attempt to forge professional relationships through non-work-related discussions.

Another avenue to pursue with day-to-day administrators is to make communication deliberate. After the daily check-in discussion with the team, set time aside to physically engage, if possible, with the other administrators to see whether they've noticed anything in order to continue to build that relationship. The local administrators will remember things during the engagement that will help enlighten some of the findings: they'll remember an old server, not on diagrams, or software used years ago but not removed, or why someone completed some action. Deliberate time with administrators gives them a safe avenue to engage where they won't feel like they're interrupting.

While the threat hunting team will most likely be visiting that network, the current administrators must continue to work there with the existing leadership. Do not demean or belittle the current administrators. It is impossible to know the context in which they were supporting the network. Painting them in a bad light will only make their job harder as they attempt to remediate any malicious actions identified. Additionally, they will be less likely to work with any future teams that they interact with.

Communicating with the adversary

You will be communicating with the adversary whether you intend to or not. Depending upon the intended adversary the hunt team is searching for, those individuals could be active on the network monitoring communication. For many advanced adversaries, it is not a big deal to pause their operations and go quiet for 3 to 6 months while they wait out a defense team. A targeted hunt is normally employed for a very finite amount of time as resources within an organization will be limited.

In all but the largest of organizations, resources will normally not be available to employ even a single individual full time to continually hunt for a specific group of adversaries. This means that a hunt team will be time bound to a specific period to search out those threat actors. Those same adversaries tend to not be constrained for completing their objectives within a specific timeline. If their current network of interest is crawling with defenders, they can hide their toolsets and their activities while they pivot over to another network to attack. Whenever those defenders appear to have left, they can return and continue on their own devious plans unhindered.

Always treat a hunt like the team is playing a game of chess or poker against a living, breathing adversary – because you are. They will react to your presence and your most insignificant actions. Everything the team does can cause a reaction from the adversary. Take this into account each step of the way and always ask, "How would the adversary perceive this and is that we would want them to think?"

Real-World Example

Several years ago, there was a security researcher that had set up a honeypot. In doing so, they were not very careful when sanitizing the system. Within minutes of a malicious actor gaining access to the system, they were able to identify the purpose of the system. We know this is not just an assumption because system logs were retrieved showing that the malicious actor reviewed the configuration files for the honeypot. Shortly after, all logs stopped as the adversary deleted all files on the system.

In this example, the security researcher was not mindful of how they were being perceived and inadvertently communicated something to their intended target. That adversary perceived the system based upon their understanding of the facts and responded accordingly.

Positive and negative non-verbal language

If communication occurs in person, or even over video, be mindful of body language as the discussion or briefing is ongoing. Body language perceptions can be different for each individual, town, city, and country. There are two general stances to look for that tend to be common across communities:

- **Closed posture**: Arms folded tightly, holding the head, stern facial expressions, avoiding looking at the presenter or the material being discussed, and head tilted back are negative signs that could convey that the individual does not agree with what is being discussed or that they are not open to receiving communication. They are firm in their perception.

- **Loose posture**: Arms open, hands loosely grasped, visual attention throughout discussions, head straight or slightly tilted to the side, and erect posture while sitting are positive signs that normally indicate that the individual is open to receiving communication.

These cues can be different based upon the cultural origins of the individual. Some research into your target audience can go a long way. Set aside your own preconceived notions of what is considered positive and negative and put your target audience first. Should you make eye contact? Are there any specific gestures or phrases that you should not use? Know your audience and understand what to expect.

Scenario A – internal threat hunt

The team lead for the new internal threat hunt team identified the first course of action for them to complete was to determine when, where, and why communication within and external to the team would need to occur. Since all members of the team were already internal to Widget Maker Inc., they'd be using a tool they already had – Slack.

The team leader set up a channel to discuss the threat hunt just inside the team. This allowed the team members to talk freely, and upon its creation, the team started chatting immediately about their excitement to work on receiving a notification from the FBI.

There was also an update channel set up for the CEO and other stakeholders who wanted to know what was happening with the team without the formality of meetings or briefings. This channel was chosen over email communications since it is easier to control the spread of messages. Therefore, it was locked down to those members on the advice of legal counsel to stop the spread of rumors and leaks that could put the organization at risk of a lawsuit or bad public relations.

The team lead also set up a channel for tips that were targeted at the other administrators and **Network Operations Center (NOC)** and **Security Operations Center (SOC)** workers. This allowed other internal agencies to assist in the threat hunt without being deeply involved in what the actual threat hunt was for.

The team lead also set aside time twice a day in the morning and early afternoon to engage directly with the threat hunting team. This would take place over company Zoom calls since a few of the members would be working from home, but would require them to have their cameras on.

The team lead set aside daily time to call the SOC and NOC managers to continue those relationships and keep them up to date with the changes that were coming. The team lead was worried the SOC and NOC would be viewed negatively given the breach that wasn't discovered. The team lead's deliberate communication was to ensure the NOC, SOC, and threat hunters were all on the same team and he would not be *throwing them under the bus* to management.

The team lead also set up regular updates to the stakeholders either in person or over a video call with cameras on. In the beginning, he had these scheduled for every 2 days but projected them to lessen as the engagement went on and the stakeholders grew confident in the team's capabilities and findings.

Scenario B – external threat hunt

CSI International had an external communication platform that they use to work as a team. They will continue to use that platform, Teams, and build a separate channel and chat to centralize communications for the organization engaged. These avenues will remain private to the team for the duration of the engagement. This will allow them to speak bluntly about findings and the situation without impacting the customer and their partners during the engagement.

Through Teams, the team lead has a separate channel built for use with the system administrator and security team. The threat hunting team lead encouraged the lead administrator and security team lead to utilize their smartphones for this communication because there are concerns the threat actor is still in the system and could be monitoring their workstations since the administrator and security team are critical members. The leaders of those sections have agreed and will be the only two to use the channel. Additionally, the team lead set aside time in the morning to call each member directly to discuss what's going on with the threat hunt and build that relationship.

The CEO demanded that updates be sent to him daily in email. The *To* list had grown to seven people and included the legal team to try and keep the threat hunt under legal privilege and avert lawsuit discovery. The team lead explained the possible threat of interception by the adversary, but the CEO and legal team wanted the timeline of performance documented for insurance purposes. The team lead was successful in getting the personal cell phone number of the CEO to communicate findings immediately upon vetting them.

The team lead had also set aside time daily in the afternoon to brief the CEO and team about the work CSI International had accomplished so far on their contract. This took place across the company's WebEx infrastructure. Right now, this was planned as an informal briefing, but it had the potential to change and require slides or other products.

With communication methods determined and engagements approved, it was time to move to the next phase of the engagement in which the team would begin to lay out their methodologies to be employed.

Summary

If you leave this chapter with nothing else, remember that communication is critical at each and every step of a threat hunt. This is not just for the team lead but for all participants. All team members (and stakeholders) must be mindful of how they are communicating verbally, non-verbally, in written form, and visually to others. Certain unintentional and minor communication complications could quickly kill any long-term standing that the team has within the organization.

Team communication can be straightforward and open. The team lead must ensure to establish the standard for how this will be carried out and then ensure the personnel follows that expectation. Operator notes are a simple and highly effective way of ensuring each analyst keeps track of what they are doing. This will keep analysts on track and enable them to provide more detailed feedback during debriefs.

When communicating with business owners, stick to the facts. If an opinion or assumption must be stated, ensure it is framed as what it is. Beyond the organization's leadership, other key stakeholders will be included in the team's daily communication. Threat hunting is exceptionally hard without the aid and support of the local network administrators. Help them out however you can and never go out of your way to make their job harder after you leave.

Finally, remember that the team will communicate with the adversary. Ensure the team is doing so in the manner and method it intends. At this point, it should be clear just how important communication is with a threat hunt. Our next step will bring us to cover various methodologies, which we will do in the next chapter. These items will cover the things that the team will need to talk about and work through to move them from initiating a hunt to preventing an adversary from achieving their objectives.

Review questions

Answer the following questions to check your knowledge of this chapter:

1. Which of the following is not a standard recipient of communication throughout the life cycle of a threat hunt? (Choose all that apply)

    A. Members of a hunt team

    B. Organizational leadership

    C. General public

    D. Adversary

    E. Network administrators

    F. Stockholders

2. Within the _____ chat channel, communication will be very fast and loose with a high degree of freedom to vocalize theories and hypotheses. This differs from the _____ chat channel, which is normally used as the primary method for the team lead to conduct and document C2 activities.

3. The first rule of interacting with a customer is to _____. This applies just as much to what is not said, as to what is said.

4. (True or false) The adversary responds to actions the hunt team takes on the network.

5. (True or false) Non-verbal postures, hand gestures, and facial expressions normally do not impact any professional relationships a hunt team would have within an organization.

Review answers

The answers to the review questions are as follows:

1. C, F. While many people may receive a report after a threat hunt, it is up to the owning organization to release it beyond the initial stakeholders participating in the threat hunt.

2. Operator, C2. The easiest way to view this is to remember that the operator channel provides the operators an open forum to discuss without worry or interference from those that might *read into* what is said.

3. State only facts. See *Communicating with business owners* for more details on why this matters.

4. True. Remember that everything a team does can, and normally will, be viewed by others including an adversary that is active on the same network. This observation is an indirect form of communication.

5. False. *Everything* an individual does or says will be interpreted as a form of communication.

5
Methodologies

So far in this book, we have been outlining the pieces that are needed to conduct a threat hunt and the environments in which they can operate. Before we learn how to execute a hunt, we need to go over some methodologies we can utilize. Regardless of what any individuals' feelings are toward any specific framework, a threat hunting team should always base its processes and organization on a methodology.

Why?

Methodologies enable teams to have repeatable processes that make sense. Frameworks and methodologies help ensure that a threat hunting team consistently aligns its efforts toward the goals and concerns of the business. Methodologies are the frameworks and structure that the details are built onto to keep the entire process aligned with what matters to the organization. They turn pure chaos into something slightly less chaotic and eventually into a highly organized system. To facilitate this transition, we will cover the general-purpose hunting cycle, the adversary methodology, and the MITRE ATT&CK Matrix.

In this chapter, we are going to cover the following topics:

- The hunting cycle
- The adversary methodology
- The MITRE ATT&CK Matrix

- Scenario A – internal threat hunt
- Scenario B – external threat hunt

By the end of the chapter, you will be able to do the following:

- *Comprehend* the different phases of a hunting cycle.
- *Discuss* common adversary attack methodologies and how they would be observed during a threat hunt.
- *Identify* the MITRE ATT&CK Matrix and how it applies to a threat hunt.

The hunting cycle

Before beginning a hunting cycle, there are a few things that need to be fully established. The threat hunters will need to understand the business needs and concerns that will be addressed throughout the life of the hunt. The scope and environment should be established with all stakeholders. Finally, the desired outcomes and deliverables should be agreed upon. Once these are in place, the team can begin its cycle.

Most of the threat hunting methodologies you can find look very similar to one another. They will all center around starting with a hypothesis or collection of hypotheses. However, this is only partly correct; a hypothesis should be driven by intelligence, awareness of the environment, and business requirements. Just because a threat hunting team identifies lateral movement on a particular portion of the network does not mean it is of significance to the team. The hypotheses for a hunt are scoped to the business requirements of the organization. If the organization is not concerned with those systems and there is no intelligence driving the hunters to that area, then it is outside the scope of what matters for *that* hunt. Take the items you gleaned from *Chapter 2, Requirements and Motivations*, and base the team's hypothesis on the business interests and concerns of the organization.

Those hypotheses should be specific enough to address the business interests and concerns, yet not so overly specific as to impede the threat hunt from addressing the organization's needs. An example of a potential hypothesis is "*The actor Fancy Bear is utilizing SMB lateral movement to move around the enterprise.*" Another example could be "*Threat actors are exploiting local administrator accounts to help exfiltrate company data from the centralized database.*" Once a sufficient list of hypotheses has been generated to fully address the organizational needs within the constraints provided, the team will identify the questions that will need to be answered to either prove or disprove the original hypothesis.

For the lateral movement hypothesis, we could ask, "*What is the baseline activity of SMB traffic on the enterprise?*" or "*What systems do not have a standard purpose of utilizing SMB traffic?*" With that new list of questions, the team must identify what data sources are required to provide answers. Moving through the process in this manner will help prevent the team from experiencing collection bias and only asking questions about datasets they know about. During this step of answering questions, the team will start building a **Collection Management Framework** (**CMF**). A CMF may contain any number of data points that are relevant to the team and the hunt.

At a minimum, the following should be utilized to provide an ample understanding of the data that's needed:

- The data type that's required to answer the question being posed by the hypothesis
- The available data sources
- The retention length of the available data
- The data owners
- The data collection methods
- The value of the data source (high/medium/low)

The following are optional but can be included to provide additional context for the team:

- Source data type
- The volume of data – estimated **events per section** (**EPS**) and size of logs
- Datasets (key:values)
- Data category (network versus host)
- Data storage location
- Cyber Kill Chain phase (a single data source may cover multiple phases)

Almost any documentation method can be utilized to generate this framework. If the team is centrally located in an area where only personnel associated with the hunt will be, then a whiteboard works great. If the team is spread out across multiple locations or if there is a concern of non-hunt personnel having access to the data, then an electronic method of documentation should be utilized. Regardless of the method, all members will need to be able to easily reference it throughout the hunt. In the following example, a spreadsheet was used to document the data and share it between all the members of the team:

Hypothesis 1 - here's where the educated guess goes that determines the required data sets					
Data Type	Data Source	Retention Length	Data Owners	Data Collection Method	Data Value
logs	webserver	24 hours	NOC	Manual	medium
logs	dns	7 days	NOC	Manual	high
logs	proxy	72 hours	NOC	Manual	medium
binary logs	exchange	45 min	NOC	Manual	high
binary logs	endpoint	variable	Security team	Manual	critical
logs	antivirus console/endpoint	90 days	Security team	Manual	critical
logs	firewall	24 hours	NOC	Manual	high
packet capture	IDS appliance	48 hours	Security team	Manual	critical
NetFlow	IDS appliance	14 days	Security team	Manual	critical

Figure 5.1 – Collection Management Framework

Once the required datasets have been identified, the team will need to do a complete review of the plan to ensure that the logic flows from the business goals and concerns through the datasets. It is important to double-check for any assumptions or areas that may have been overlooked. It is much easier to adjust a plan at this stage than it is in the middle of the threat hunt. Additional resources, such as tools, personnel, or timeline adjustments, are much easier to integrate from the beginning than halfway through the hunt. If everything is in order, then it is time to get the team's plan for the upcoming hunt approved. Depending on the organization, this could be the team lead or even the customer requesting the hunt. The purpose of receiving approval is continuing communication. It is extremely valuable to have all the stakeholders on the same page regarding what will be conducted, when it will be occurring, and why it is happening. It will give everyone a chance to raise any concerns before execution or address any lagging areas.

Once everything has been approved and the time for execution has arrived, everyone should be ready to begin and never look back. Right?

This is incorrect. While executing the threat hunt and once the hunt has finished, feedback should be retrieved in the form of debriefs. This is not the constant feedback that analysts should be providing to leadership as events unfold. This is the end-of-day and end-of-mission feedback. For anyone that has not participated in these debriefing sessions, know that it is not uncommon for people to be outspoken. Let's look at some general rules of engagement that you should follow. The team lead should adjust this list to fit their leadership, not management, style.

There are certain rules of engagement that should always be followed for all debriefs. Just like the mandatory fields for the CMF listed previously, the following must be in place before you begin. Always adjust additional rules based on the personalities within the team:

- Position, length of time on the team, and any other differentiators do not matter.

- Each individual has an equal voice.

- No personal attacks.

- Call the issue what it is. Do not attempt to word it nicely or talk around an issue.

- When you're addressing concerns, always start with the actions and performance of the leadership.

> **Note**
>
> **Radical transparency** is defined as actions that will drastically promote openness within an organization.
>
> When addressing any negative actions for a certain period, it is highly recommended that you start with how leadership has performed. Keep in mind that this mindset only works if the teams' culture is not contrary to this manner of extremely direct discussion. If your team has members that this method does not work for, do not force it! For those teams who are open to more candid and direct conversation, starting with leadership will set the tone for everyone else. The concept of leading with *radical transparency* is taking hold in more cyber organizations as it can strengthen the level of trust throughout the organization, from the bottom to the top, well beyond anything that has been experienced over the past several decades.

For an end-of-day debrief, the order of events will begin with a timeline reconstruction (recall those operator notes from *Chapter 4, Communication Breakdown*). You will learn more about the end-of-mission deberief and feedback in *Chapter 13, Post Hunt Activity and Maturing a Team*. Build a relative timeline of the significant events that occurred from the start of the shift. As the timeline is being generated by the team, anything of note that needs to be addressed will be called out and annotated for discussion later. Next, the lead will start identifying anything good/bad that occurred that wasn't placed on the timeline.

After that, it is time to talk about what happened. Dig into the day and figure out what happened, good or bad, and why. Did leadership make a bad decision? If so, everyone saw it, so talk about it and how it will be prevented in the future. Did the analyst find the adversary? If so, what did they do to identify the indicator and what does everyone else need to do to pivot off this new information? The final piece will be the documentation for this debrief. Hopefully, the lead assigned someone to write it down as it was happening and talked through the plan for the following shift.

At the end of each shift, this debrief should be followed up with a quick review of the following day's activities to allow the team to adjust any planned actions based on the new information that's been identified. This final step completes the execution cycle that the team goes through at the end of their shift. The following is a summary of each step of this simple execution cycle:

- **Prebrief**: This briefing will be conducted before *any work* for the shift begins. Any turnover from the previous shift or note reviews should have already been conducted. The goal will be to ensure that the team leader and their members are on the same page as far as what that day's priorities are, as well as pass on any specific pieces of information that might be of high importance. This could be something as simple as a distinguished visitor stopping by later or even an adversary being identified in the shift before. By doing this, the priorities for the day will be adjusted to focus on the new indicators.

- **Execution**: This phase is exactly what it sounds like – the hunt mission is being executed either on or off the network. During this phase, all the operators should be taking notes of what actions are occurring and the things they have observed.

- **Debrief**: This is when, at the end of the shift, all the members review what took place in that shift, mentioned anything good or bad that happened, and discuss the path forward. If operations are occurring in a 24-hour cycle, this phase should not be joined with the next shift's prebrief. This will be a distinct phase for the outgoing shift to recap everything that happened. The next shift can listen in but should not participate.

- **Adjust Plan**: Hypotheses, assumptions, and expectations change throughout the hunt. Some things should remain rigid, such as the hypothesis that is being pursued. However, certain things can be adjusted daily based on any new information that's provided. An example would be adjusting how data is reviewed based on new intel that was discovered that provided insight into additional tactics that the adversary performs.

The following diagram shows the execution cycle and its different steps:

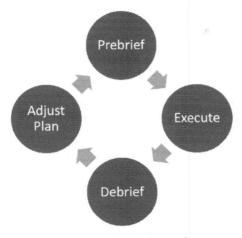

Figure 5.2 – Execution cycle

The end-of-mission debrief is conducted similarly to the end-of-day debrief and is normally a giant reiteration of all of the end-of-day debriefs; it covers the big milestones that could not be remediated during the hunt. During the end-of-mission debrief, the items that improve the team are normally identified and the ways to instill them are put into practice. It's important to ensure that any areas that are identified for improvement, along with the recommended improvement actions, are assigned directly to someone that will be able to implement them. If this final step isn't executed, then the team will inevitably experience the same shortcomings over and over again.

This final debrief can be observed in the following hunting cycle diagram. Each hunt will follow this path, regardless of how many times the team has operated on that particular network. As the team and owning network organization mature, some phases will shorten, but they will still be performed:

- **Purpose Generation**: During this phase, the reason behind the threat hunt is generated. No idea or endeavor should go beyond this phase unless the threat hunt can be tied directly to the organizational priorities and/or goals.

- **Planning**: This phase will answer the *how* of the threat hunt. A hypothesis will be generated to provide insight into something that is tied directly to the organization's priorities. This hypothesis will then allow the members to identify what is required to answer those questions.

- **Plan Stress Testing**: Very rarely will a plan work flawlessly as initially planned. This phase will allow all stakeholders to perform a *tabletop exercise* of the plan to generate various *what-if* scenarios to see how the plan would hold up under stress.

- **Approval**: Once a plan has been designed, it is time to gain approval from the organization's leadership.

- **Execution**: The approved plan will be conducted by the threat hunting team within the scope that's been authorized.

- **Debrief**: With the execution phase completed, all prior events will be reviewed to analyze how well everything was performed at each step. This will allow the long-term performance of both the threat hunting team and the organization to be improved.

The following diagram shows the hunting cycle and all its different phases:

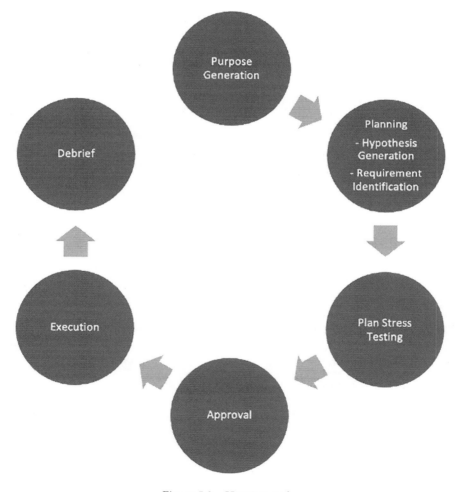

Figure 5.3 – Hunting cycle

While each hunting mission will be unique, they should always follow the same cycle of identifying the purpose, planning, testing that plan, obtaining written approval, executing those planned activities, and reviewing what happened. There will be two execution cycles – one for the overarching mission and a daily cycle that all members should go through. With this cycle established for the hunters, we can look at the process the adversaries utilize.

The adversary methodology

Just like having a framework to cycle through, from conception to completion, to identify threats is a must-have, employing a common adversary methodology framework within a team needs to be set. This particular method involves the steps that an adversary takes to compromise the environment and complete their objective. The most common model that's used is the Lockheed Martin Cyber Kill Chain, as shown in the following diagram:

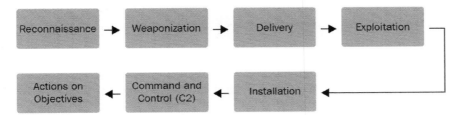

Figure 5.4 – Cyber Kill Chain

This particular kill chain is simply a chain that the adversary *builds* as they perform offensive actions. With each step, a new link is added. If they get to the end, then they have achieved their goal, whatever it may be, and are considered successful. This typically means that the cyber defenders have not been successful and that the business's information system confidentiality, integrity, or availability has been compromised. From a defensive standpoint, the kill chain turns into something rather simple and helps defenders visualize what needs to be done.

For example, if the organization concentrates on delivery and installation to the point that an adversary is unable to move past those areas, this means that the defenders have been successful in their goals. An adversary *must* complete each link. But why does this matter from a threat hunting perspective? Knowing where the adversary is and what they are trying to achieve can provide the hunter with the opportunity to get ahead of them. Most threat hunting activities will not observe the reconnaissance and weaponization phases at all. The delivery and exploitation phases will normally be identified as secondary artifacts and not the initial indicators. Finally, the installation, **Command and Control (C2)**, and actions on objectives phases are where threat hunters will spend most of their time searching for **indicators of compromise (IoCs)**.

From the adversary's perspective, this particular kill chain is accurate, as well as widely utilized, in the cyber defense community. The issue that threat hunters will run into is that it will need to be customized to the network that the hunt is being conducted on. Two such examples are the Expanded Cyber Kill Chain, which is developed by Sean Malone (the original graphic can be found at Sean's website at `https://www.seantmalone.com/research/`), and the ICS Cyber Kill Chain, which is developed by Rob Lee. The following diagram shows the Expanded Cyber Kill Chain:

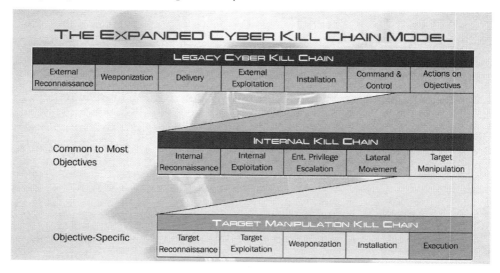

Figure 5.5 – Expanded Cyber Kill Chain, as designed by Sean Malone

This kill chain is unique in that it aids in correcting an oversimplification that can be experienced in the Lockheed Martin Cyber Kill Chain. Between link 6, **Command and Control**, and link 7, **Actions on Objectives**, a lot of activities are happening. It is very rare for an adversary to immediately compromise a single system and not need to do anything else on the network. Most of the time, after this initial exploitation of a network, an adversary will conduct reconnaissance on a network and escalate their span of control. Eventually, they will identify the true target they need to access. Once they are on that system, they will perform another set of actions.

Under the Expanded Cyber Kill Chain, each of these is a unique sub-chain. The first chain allows an adversary to gain persistent access to a network. Once that has been established, they will work on the second sub-chain, which gives them access to the network. The final sub-chain covers the actions that need to be taken to meet their goals. If the adversary is on the second chain and the defensive team can *break* their initial installation method (link 5), then it will have no major effect on the adversary. The defenders must move ahead of the adversary on the correct chain to prevent them from completing their objectives.

This kill chain was developed to address some of the unique situations that can be found in **operational technology** (**OT**) networks. It acknowledges that most attacks will be initiated through the standard **information technology** (**IT**) networks and follow the Lockheed Martin Cyber Kill Chain. Once that chain has been completed, another chain will be completed that's unique to the OT environment.

In these types of environments, generic offensive toolsets will very rarely work for what the adversary requires. This means that the targeted attack will have to go through a design phase that's unique to that network and the equipment on it. This creates a unique development and testing phase during ICS attack cycles. These two links in the kill chain can be extremely long since the attackers are preparing unique code and programs for the attack. Once an attack has occurred, it is not uncommon to see a large gap in activity from when the IT network was compromised to when the actions on objectives were completed on the OT network.

The MITRE ATT&CK Matrix

The MITRE ATT&CK Matrix was originally designed to address several growing concerns in the cyber security community. Overall, there was a need to address adversarial behavior with a common lexicon at an appropriate depth that was meaningful to defenders. While methodology frameworks such as the Lockheed Martin Cyber Kill Chain work, they are very high level and generic. The MITRE ATT&CK Matrix addresses this lagging issue in detail.

With its 14 different categories, otherwise known as tactics, this Matrix provides insight into each of the actions an adversary could go through while performing their intrusion. For threat hunters, this Matrix can be critical in helping narrow down the scope and tactics that are required for a hunt. Intel analysts can utilize this Matrix in conjunction with another MITRE tool, called Navigator, in which you can overlay an adversary's known capabilities on top of the ATT&CK Matrix to find out what needs to be focused on next. An organization can take this a step further and combine this with many known defensive capabilities to create a heat map of where they do not have adequate coverage against certain threat actors or attack vectors.

To make this even easier to comprehend, we can lay all of this out in one sentence: adversaries use various **tactics, techniques, and procedures** (**TTPs**) to perform their activities. A comprehensive list of all of the various tactics and techniques that are utilized is listed on the MITRE ATT&CK Matrix. An update-to-date listing of the MITRE ATT&CK Matrix can be found at `https://attack.mitre.org`. At the time of writing, these tactics, followed by their MITRE IDs, are as follows:

- **Reconnaissance (TA0043)**: The adversary is gathering information to use for further events.

- **Resource Development (TA0042)**: The adversary is establishing resources to use for its follow-on attacks. This can range from acquiring hardware, additional access, or purchasing already compromised accounts.

- **Initial Access (TA0001)**: The adversary is attempting to gain initial access to the organization's system(s).

- **Execution (TA0002)**: The adversary is attempting to run malicious code on the organization's system(s). Note that malicious code does not have to be anything destructive – it could simply be code that provides the adversary with better insight into how the internal network is constructed.

- **Persistence (TA0003)**: The adversary is implementing mechanisms to retain access to the organization's network.

- **Privilege Escalation (TA0004)**: Very rarely does the adversary land on the exact system with the access they require to achieve their goals. At this stage, they will attempt to gain access to the system(s) and/or permissions that they need to achieve their objectives.

- **Defense Evasion (TA0005)**: The adversary is attempting to avoid being found by any of the local defenders.

- **Credential Access (TA0006)**: The adversary is attempting to expand its list of compromised accounts and/or passwords.

- **Discovery (TA0007)**: The adversary is conducting internal reconnaissance on how the enterprise is employed.

- **Lateral Movement (TA0008)**: The adversary is attempting to move through the enterprise to other systems.

- **Collection (TA0009)**: The adversary is gathering data that aligns with its interests and goals.

- **Command and Control (TA0011)**: The adversary is attempting to communicate with compromised systems to gain control of their behavior.

- **Exfiltration (TA0010)**: The adversary is attempting to move the collected data off the network.

- **Impact (TA0040)**: The adversary is attempting to manipulate the behavior of the systems and/or data. This could include modifying or destroying the data, or interrupting a system's availability.

All of these tactics have numerous techniques that can be employed. For example, the *Initial Access* tactic has nine techniques currently listed under it:

- Drive-by Compromise
- Exploit Public-Facing Application
- External Remote Services
- Hardware Additions
- Phishing
- Replication Through Removable Media
- Supply Chain Compromise
- Trusted Relationship
- Valid Accounts

Each of these techniques can be drilled into to help identify the procedures that are listed by specific adversaries (if there is one), various mitigation strategies, and detection locations, which, at the time of writing, are referred to as data sources.

For example, if we were interested in the *Dragonfly* cyber espionage group (G00035), we would see that MITRE has an initial access technique of theirs listed as **Drive-by Compromise (T1189)**. This technique should be able to be detected in various **application logs (DS0015)**, **file creation logs (DS0022)**, and **network traffic logs (DS0029)**. Researching any of those three MITRE Detection IDs would provide a hunt team with additional insight into what and where to begin searching for the technique that was utilized by that threat actor. The following diagram depicts this flow:

Figure 5.6 – How adversaries are linked to the MITRE ATT&CK Matrix

This list of tactics and techniques can be combined with the ATT&CK Navigator. The Navigator Matrix allows an organization to overlay its tactics and techniques over its detection capabilities. This will generate a *heat map* to show where the organization can detect techniques, along with areas where techniques would go undetected. A threat hunting team can utilize this knowledge to potentially deploy sensors to fill in knowledge gaps and detect adversaries in places they had previously been able to roam freely.

This group of tools is well worth the time and effort an organization can put forth. They should learn how to utilize them properly and begin integrating them into the teams' cycles. They will help refine the teams' processes and minimize wasted resources.

Now that we have discussed a handful of the different methodologies that are employed by hunt teams, cyber defenders, and adversaries, let's learn how these items are put into practice. No two teams or scenarios are the same. They will always be molded to their particular use case while adhering to the general structure the methodology provides.

Scenario A – internal threat hunt

The team has been formed and with the Cyber Security Framework and ongoing discussions completed, the team has decided on which methodology to use. Two main areas influenced this decision. The first is the fact that the FBI has in-depth data on the threat actor that was provided to the team. The second is the fact that the threat actor is not concerned with short-term gains and has been known to conduct attack campaigns that are measured in years rather than hours or days. With these items in mind, the MITRE ATT&CK Matrix has been chosen as the methodology the team will use to test hypotheses.

The team lead takes the information from the FBI – phishing emails, beaconing to IPs, and more – and selects them in the ATT&CK Matrix to determine what datasets are necessary to hunt the threat actor. Additional datasets will need to be picked by the team, but here is a curtailed list of the ones that are the most important to their environment:

- Initial Access:
  - Phishing: Spear phishing attachment
  - ID: T1566.001
  - Dataset: Email logs and proxy logs
- Execution:
  - Command and Scripting Interpreter: PowerShell
  - ID: T1059.001
  - Dataset: Host logs for PowerShell
- Persistence:
  - Create Account: Local account
  - Create Account: Domain account
  - ID: T1136.001
  - ID: T1136.002
  - Dataset: Host logs and domain controller logs

- Privilege Escalation:

  - Valid Accounts: Local accounts

  - Valid Accounts: Domain accounts

  - ID: T1078.003

  - ID: T1078.002

  - Dataset: Host logs and domain controller logs

- Command and Control:

  - Application Layer Protocol: Web protocols

  - ID: T1071.001

  - Dataset: Network logs, proxy logs, and firewall logs

With the scope narrowed down, the hunt team can focus on just a few attack points that the threat actor is known to employ. Doing so will greatly increase the team's success while minimizing any disruption that's caused by the team chasing down errant activity that's not related to the hunt.

Scenario B – external threat hunt

The team has been formed and with the Cyber Security Framework and ongoing discussions completed, the team has decided on which methodology to use. Because of the lack of ongoing security controls and a comprehensive policy, they have chosen the Lockheed Martin Cyber Kill Chain as the easiest to adapt by **Cyber Security Intelligence** (**CSI**) for the client.

CSI, the system administrators, and the security team review the CSF and start annotating where data would be located to provide visibility into each of the sections of the Lockheed Martin Cyber Kill Chain. Here is an abbreviated list, and the sample CMF as it applies to CSI's client:

- **Reconnaissance**: Web servers, DNS logs, and proxy logs

- **Weaponization**: Darknet intel on the vendors that the client uses

- **Delivery**: The email logs and proxy logs to be downloaded

- **Exploitation**: The endpoint logs, antivirus logs, and software logs for the systems that are critical to the business

- **Installation**: The endpoint logs and antivirus logs

- **Command and Control**: The network logs, proxy logs, and DNS logs
- **Action on Objectives**: The endpoint logs and network logs (NetFlow/packet)

By utilizing the Cyber Kill Chain, the team has been able to narrow down the scope of what will matter to them as the hunt begins. From here, they will work with the local defenders and network administrators to identify which items can easily be obtained while providing the largest coverage of the kill chain. For example, the endpoint logs span three different links in the kill chain, but they might be difficult to obtain. At the same time, the proxy and DNS logs also cover three links in the chain but they are readily available. As such, those items will be at the top of the priority list for the team to obtain.

Summary

A purposeful and repeatable hunting cycle methodology is needed for a threat hunt team. Always build a hypothesis for a hunt off of business requirements and concerns; never build them off of the known datasets that are available. At the same time, ensure that you utilize a collection management framework to help the team choose the resources that are required to conduct an effective threat hunt.

Daily and post-hunt debriefs must occur if the team is to overcome obstacles and improve. Honesty and candid discussions will need to occur during these events. Visualization methods can work wonders throughout this entire process, so use the one that fits the environment and the teams' processes. Whatever is chosen, ensure that the entire team is using the same one. Finally, the MITRE ATT&CK Matrix can be leveraged in many different ways. Educate the team and organization on its employment as early as possible.

If it was not already clear from the previous chapters, a successful threat hunt requires more than a cyber analyst. A critical piece of the hunt will be the intelligence ingestion cycle and the intel analysts that control it. In the next chapter, we will answer the ever-present question of *why do you need those extra resources for intel?*

Review questions

Answer the following questions to check your knowledge of this chapter:

1. Which of the following are phases of the hunting cycle? (Choose all that apply)

   A. Planning

   B. Obtaining approval

   C. Research

   D. Execution

2. True or false: The execution cycle should be restarted each shift.

3. According to the Expanded Cyber Kill Chain, how many unique chain types will an attack have?

4. What is the high-level difference between the Lockheed Martin Cyber Kill Chain and the MITRE ATT&CK Matrix?

Review answers

The answers to the review questions are as follows:

1. A, B, D

2. True

3. Three (Legacy Cyber Kill Chain, Internal Kill Chain, and Target Manipulation Kill Chain)

4. The Lockheed Martin Cyber Kill Chain is process-oriented, while the MITRE ATT&CK Matrix focuses on the technical nature of the attack.

6

Threat Intelligence

This chapter has been included in an attempt to drive a straightforward concept home for all of you – intelligence matters! Without the inclusion of intelligence and intelligence analysts in a threat hunt, the entire effort will be severely hamstrung throughout the course of the hunt. It would be no different than trying to ride a tricycle that only has two wheels – it just does not work well.

In this chapter, we are going to cover the following topics:

- Types of intelligence
- Why intel matters
- Visualization model
- Threat intelligence feeds
- Scenario A—internal threat hunt
- Scenario B—external threat hunt

By the end of the chapter, you will be able to do the following:

- *Identify* the different types of intel that could be applied to a threat hunt.
- *Comprehend* the importance of intelligence during a hunt.
- *Comprehend* how intelligence can be applied to a team throughout a hunt.

Types of intelligence

Before going too deep, we need to cover the main types of threat intelligence available today.

Strategic threat intelligence is a high-level concept of intelligence that covers an actor's motivations and intentions and potentially their capabilities. It will not get into the low-level details of *how* something is accomplished. Instead, this intelligence is the *why* behind the campaigns that threat actors execute on their victims.

This type of intelligence is great for ingestion at the managerial and leadership levels. A technical background is not typically required, yet it can still easily be correlated with the organizational priorities at large.

Operational threat intelligence is a context-rich version of intelligence that contains detailed information on things such as forensic analysis of toolsets and an adversary's known **tactics, techniques, and procedures (TTPs)**. This intelligence is the *how* and *what* of a threat actor's campaign. There will be many different operational reports on the same threat actors as they modify their tactics, start new campaigns, and deal with repercussions from their activities. Anyone that has read a technical report of an intrusion could recognize that report as a source of operational threat intelligence.

When conducting a threat hunt, both of these types of intelligence will be necessary. Strategic threat intelligence can give you a high-level view of an intrusion and assist in aligning the threat hunt requirements with business needs. Operational threat intelligence tells the analyst *what* to hunt for.

Why intel matters

A threat intelligence analyst will ensure a steady stream of intelligence into and out of the threat hunting team. Directly out of the gate, intel analysts will be responsible for providing target-specific intelligence to aid in the planning and execution of the threat hunt. This could be anything from details on generic threats that the organization is concerned about to reports on targeted intrusions that have been carried out. This information can aid in understanding the specific TTPs an adversary would utilize. Additionally, it has the potential to shed light on potential intentions, motivations, and responses to hunt activity.

Throughout the execution of the hunt, the intel analyst will be responsible for fulfilling **requests for information (RFIs)** as well as enriching any data highlighted by the team. RFIs can range from clarification on a threat actor's capabilities to the history of protocols involved in past attacks. The scope of what the team lead will want the RFIs constrained to will be based upon the experience level of the analyst assigned.

Data enrichment is one of the larger areas an intel analyst shines in as a force multiplier for the team. Once the team has identified a piece of data or dataset that they believe is relevant, intel can be used to enhance this data beyond the initial understanding of it. This differs from the collection performed by hunt analysts as those individuals should only be searching for surface-level information that might take a few minutes to discover and report, whereas an intel analyst can spend multiple shifts digging through various databases looking at a single piece of information and tying all that information together to provide a deep context to what the data means and the impact it has on the threat hunt.

Finally, all of this intelligence that has been collected, tailored, and organized throughout the hunt can be utilized to produce an adversary threat report at the completion of the hunt. This is not a mandatory product but is a common request by an organization that does not possess their own intelligence capability.

Real-World Example

Threat analysts have used open source intelligence in the past and produced astounding results. One such example is a security researcher that analyzed various malware sets and attempted to categorize them. There was a particular piece of malware that did not behave or contain any similar source code to other malware that they had analyzed. As such, it was considered an anomaly and the intention of the maker was unknown.

Upon closer inspection into its behavior and how it compared with other malicious code that had been analyzed, a commonality was identified. This particular piece of malware contained command and control information that was registered in the same manner as a different family of malware. Due to this very specific commonality, the analyst was able to conclude that this unique software was, in fact, an unknown variant of a well-known threat actor's toolset. Without the use of intelligence and intelligence analysis, this critical connection would never have been made.

Visualization model

In the real-world example mentioned in the previous section, an analyst was able to pinpoint commonalities between different toolsets to show where they overlapped. The diamond model (as shown in *Figure 6.1*), developed by Sergio Caltagirone, Andrew Pendergast, and Christopher Betz, provides the ability to do this if utilized to its full extent. This model has been widely adopted across the cybersecurity community to the point that it appears in numerous **security information and event management (SIEM)** systems and threat hunting software to aid in the identification of malicious activity:

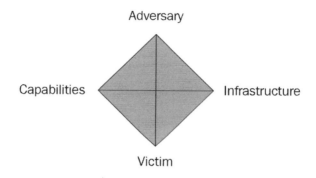

Figure 6.1 – Diamond model

When utilizing this model, understand that each event will have its own diamond. In each node (corner), any known information will need to be displayed. Some events will have very little that will be known, while for others, there might be a mountain of data. Once a model is developed, an analyst can begin pivoting off of the known data in each area to expand upon unknown items. Maybe there is a known command and control mechanism that communicates through DNS queries. Those DNS servers could be a part of the threat actor's infrastructure. Are they used for any other malware sets or belong to a known threat actor? The connection between multiple datasets could be as simple as two DNS entries created on the same day or registered by the same individual. These are the rabbit holes that the analyst can spend hours upon hours going down to flush out.

Definitions

Indicator of compromise: A piece of data, commonly found in logs, which shows potential malicious activity on an enterprise or system.

When an intel analyst and threat hunting team has matured, this model will become second nature to them. It will be possible to overlay this model onto others, such as the Lockheed Martin Cyber Kill Chain, and create activity threads for multiple intrusion sets. This level of insight is what allows a threat hunting team to gain the advantage and move ahead of an adversary.

Threat intelligence feeds

At a certain point, it will become obvious that no group of intel analysts can be experts in all the things that are constantly evolving in the intelligence community. There is simply too much information out there for any single group of individuals to be constantly up to date on the evolving threat landscape. Therefore, it is very important to ensure that the team is able to use targeted threat intelligence feeds and products.

There are numerous free and paid intelligence products on the market for individuals or organizations to subscribe to. Each can result in materials such as monthly or quarterly threat reports for the entire cybersecurity community, databases that can be queried, summaries of threat actor discussions on forums, and even live feeds that can be ingested into an organization's SIEM or network defenses for near real-time correlation of activities and increased protection. Similar to the rule of thumb for logging, intelligence is only as good as the organization that does something with it. If an organization spends thousands of dollars on access to threat feeds and then never monitors or otherwise utilizes them, it will be resources wasted.

However, if they are of interest, understand that there isn't a lot of difference between paid and free subscriptions. It is possible to identify some high-value content from free threat feeds for unique sectors such as industrial control systems and operational technology. The main downside that the organization could experience is understanding that as the intelligence feed is free, it will typically allow anyone to provide data. The quality of data might be lower than one that is based on a paid subscription. Additionally, with paid subscriptions, an organization will normally have a *members-only* section in which they get access early or access to trusted intelligence that is not released to the public.

For a threat hunting team, it is highly recommended to research the available feeds for the team's targeted enterprise and consider including them. When doing so, be sure to take into account whether the analysis of intelligence will occur on the team's systems or someone else's. Utilizing sources such as VirusTotal is great for checking known malicious malware. However, if an analyst uploads a file to the VirusTotal system, that file and everything it contains will be available for review by anyone with the appropriate subscription to that database. Many companies have lost proprietary and sensitive information this way.

A more private solution called *sandboxes* can be deployed within an organization to provide this type of function without the inclusion of a third party. These products can be easily found in a variety of different configurations and capabilities and are available in both a free and paid model. Depending upon the product(s) employed, they can give a similar type of feedback available from the public VirusTotal but without the worry of sharing data with a third party. This will be covered in more depth in *Chapter 9, Hardware and Toolsets*.

Scenario A – internal threat hunt

With the identification of some hypotheses and data logs, information is available to research before the threat hunt happens by an intel analyst. This role is a requirement of the team, and the team lead speaks with the CEO and stakeholders about how best to fill this position moving forward.

The CEO wants to keep the threat hunting team organic but doesn't want to commit to another manned position until the team has shown it can accomplish the goals set for it. So, they will approve a contract position to supply the intel analysis role for the initial hunt and then, based on the outcome, a full-time hireable one.

The team lead works quickly with HR and their team to get referrals and hires for a contract position that will be filled quickly enough to get the work done. Thankfully, one of the team members has a friend who's done intel in the past and is looking to get back into the discipline.

Because of the lack of investment in intel, the only items of use are the old personas the intel contract analyst has on some darknet forums and the free intelligence feeds. Utilizing basic information such as the company's domains, external IP addresses, executives, and notable engineers, the intel analyst begins their search. After a few hours, they've identified a little bit of chatter related to the external IPs and a couple of the senior engineers. This information is relayed to the team lead.

Scenario B – external threat hunt

CSI has a subcontract with an intelligence firm called IntelAllSense Inc. Throughout the hunt, the team lead works with stakeholders, hypothesis development, and data source determination until they've built a portfolio of items for the contractors to check on. They pass the company's domains, external IP addresses, the enterprise's global address list, and selected social media profiles from critical workers.

IntelAllSense has access to long-running personas on the darknet that threat actors trust. This access is in many extortion, fraud, and hacking sales forums and Telegram groups. They also have access to aggregation tools and network monitoring tools that are automatically enriched with intelligence data by the tool developers. These tools are very expensive, but because IntelAllSense sells these services, the costs are spread among client contracts, which makes it possible for smaller firms such as CSI to use them.

Additionally, the team lead asks for searches for industrial espionage services to be conducted on the darknet with reference to the organization requiring help. Finally, the team lead works with IntelAllSense to determine who would be the on-call analyst during the hunt and fulfilling the RFI requests that resulted from hunting activities.

With the intel analyst position secured, the team lead reads them into the current process phase and prepares them for working with the team remotely.

Summary

In this chapter, we learned how useful strategic threat intelligence is for a non-technical audience and how it gives everyone the *why*. Operational threat intelligence is useful for a technical audience and tells the analyst *what* to hunt for. Intelligence and intelligence analysts can provide answers to RFIs, data enrichment, and deliverables requested by an organization. These analysts and the information they provide are a must-have resource on any threat hunt – always include them as a critical component of the team.

The diamond model can provide much-needed visualization and the capability of pivoting off of single datasets. Train intel and hunt analysts on the partnership and how to communicate, as well as pivoting off of the data each provides to the other.

Intelligence feeds can be a great addition to the automation of data analysis as well as the correlation of information. Be mindful and selective of threat feeds to minimize *noise* that intel and hunt analysts will have to work through.

If nothing else is taken away from this chapter, remember this:

Include intelligence and intelligence analysts in all threat hunts!

At this point, all of the foundational concepts have been outlined for what is needed to conduct a threat hunt. In the next chapter, we will step through the processes of planning a hunt in order to successfully meet business objectives while minimizing thrash experienced by the team.

Review questions

Answer the following questions to check your knowledge of this chapter:

1. Which of the following is not a type of threat intelligence? (Choose all that apply)

    A.   Strategic

    B.   Orientation

    C.   Operational

    D.   General

2. Is it possible to conduct a threat hunt without intel?

3. What happens if intel is not included?

Review answers

The answers to the review questions are as follows:

1. B, D. The main two types of intelligence are Strategic (high-level) and Operational (detailed and/or technical).

2. Yes. While it is very possible, it is not recommended as intelligence will act as a force multipler for the hunt.

3. The effectiveness of the hunt is greatly reduced.

7
Planning

At this point, every piece that is required for a successful threat hunt has been identified. Now it is time to put all of the pieces together. In doing so, the team will quickly move from thinking *we really need to do this* to a place that will allow them to say *we did this right*.

In *Chapter 5, Methodologies*, the hunting cycle was discussed with the starting point of identifying requirements. These are the business needs and concerns that are the origin of the threat hunt. What are the items that the organizational leadership is concerned with? What are the network administrators and defenders seeing that is of concern? What is being targeted online that is similar to our organization? Is there a critical software vulnerability in some dependency the organization might be using?

All of these items should be prioritized and approved by the requesting organization. The goal is to start planning with all the stakeholders on the same page as far as what the requirements are and their associated priorities.

In this chapter, we are going to cover the following topics:

- Restraints and constraints
- Defining the scope
- Defining "bad"
- Assumptions
- Success factors
- Planned triggers

- Identifying resources required

- Communication contracts

- Reviewing and stress testing the plan

- Approving the plan

- Scenario A—internal threat hunt

- Scenario B—external threat hunt

By the end of the chapter, you will be able to do the following:

- *Discuss* the phases of a planning cycle.

- *Comprehend* the differences between restraints and constraints.

- *Discuss* the importance that communication plays within the planning cycle.

- *Comprehend* how to define a scope and identify the resources required.

Restraints and constraints

Before attempting to identify team constructs and the equipment that they will need, the listing of restraints, constraints, and then assumptions needs to start.

Moving on to the threat hunt, the team should already have a listing of actions or events that they do not want to occur. All these items are restraints since the team is forcing itself into not doing something. Restraints aren't immutable; the team can change them as needed. Some common examples are listed as follows:

- An external threat hunt team will hand off any *legal* activity to local defenders if law enforcement is involved in the target enterprise.

- The team will not provide definitive intention or association for any activity that occurs on the enterprise.

- The team will not provide unsanitized examples or reports from previous threat hunts.

- The customer organization is responsible for any new configurations and the implementation of defensive actions within the enterprise.

- The team will not be responsible for remediation actions.

- The team will only hunt on certain types of networks that they are experienced and trained on.

Once all of the restraints have been listed, the constraints will be identified. Constraints might be applied by the organization. Additionally, they might be legal requirements or even cultural if the threat hunt is taking place in a foreign land. Some common examples are listed as follows:

- What is the authorized scope of the threat hunt? And does that align with the requirements?
- What is the authorized time frame for the threat hunt? And does that align with the proposed scope?
- Is there a limitation on the number of personnel involved? And does this align with the proposed time frame and scope?
- Can these constraints be modified during the threat hunt? And by whom?
- Who is the team allowed to interface with?
- Can the team remove any data from the network? Can data leave the building that it came from? Is that data allowed to leave the country of origin or must it stay within those geographic boundaries?
- Can the team utilize their own equipment?
- Can the threat hunt be local to the organization?
- Is there a required background check requirement for access to the network or facility?
- Is there a language (for example, English, Spanish, or Japanese) requirement?
- Is the threat hunt intended to be publicized in some fashion?

It takes time for the initial restraints and constraints to be effectively communicated between the requesting organization and the threat hunting team. By the end of that coordination, each stakeholder should have a firm idea of what will be authorized and what is out of bounds for the team. All of this information will be utilized to fully define our next area of concern, that is, the scope of the hunt.

Defining the scope

With the restraints and constraints listed, the idea of the scope of the threat hunt should be clear. The team will need to take the time to formalize and acknowledge, in writing, the proposed scope of the threat hunt. The extra communication will be utilized at each step of the hunt to ensure there's no confusion between the stakeholders and the team. Additionally, this will ensure that any contractual disagreements are rectified early on.

When documenting the scope, it should include a listing of the systems and networks that the team will be hunting on. If the organization says that they would like the team to hunt across their production network, then this network should be, at minimum, listed by name. If there is an enclave that is attached to that network, that enclave could be included by name. This is a great time to begin establishing the collection management framework, as outlined in *The hunting cycle* section of *Chapter 5, Methodologies*.

The same process will be accomplished for determining items that are out of scope. Networks that the threat hunt team should not interact with should be identified, at a minimum by name, and annotated on the scoping document. For example, if there is a credit card processing network that the hunt team cannot interact with due to the PCI DSS standards requirements, it needs to be listed as a no-go network.

With each item identified for the inclusion or the explicit exclusion of the scope, the team will need to conduct a sanity check. Does this inclusion or exclusion negatively impact the hunt, or does it prevent the team from addressing the business requirements driving the hunt? If it does, then return to the reason for identifying the item and address why it was listed in the area it was. There will be times when an organization will have a requirement or need, but will not want to provide the resources required to address it. This has to be communicated upfront, with the impacts and risks made clear to the stakeholders and in the documentation of the final outcome.

Once the scope has been formalized in the approved hunt plan, it should not be modified. Understand that this is a restraint and not a hard limitation. It is a good idea to outline a process in the hunt plan that the team and customer can accomplish if all stakeholders are willing and able to adjust the scope during the hunt. Two common areas to outline are those who can approve the modifications and what events, or priorities, would warrant consideration for scope modification. A very common occurrence for contingencies such as this is when something unexpected, but very *bad*, has been found that would cause a bigger business impact than what was originally being hunted for. Understanding what these things are is exactly the topic of our next section: what is *bad*, and how does a team know if what they find matters to them?

Defining "bad"

Thresholds need to be established, along with appropriate triggers, regarding how and when to consider that the collected evidence is interesting enough for an analyst to dig deeper into or when it should be handed off to local defenders to follow up. This should be based upon the organization's threshold and level of risk acceptance, along with the defined purpose of the threat hunt. While a data point that is observed could clearly be of a malicious nature, if it does not pose a suitable risk to the organization and does not align with the intention of the hunt, then it will not meet the definition of "bad" as far as the threat hunters are concerned. All of these ideas and considerations should be defined within the hunt plan.

> **Real-World Example**
>
> During a threat hunt, a team was reviewing network traffic and was seeing communication traffic between internal hosts and a few different known botnets. While this is most definitely malicious and interesting to an analyst, it was not within their scope of things to search for. The lead was able to communicate these items back to the owning organization and pass all the relevant information off to the local defenders for investigation and remediation. After this, the analyst tuned their equipment to ignore this particular type of activity. This ensured that the hunt team's resources were not taken up with actions that did not pertain to their primary objective and were more likely to be successful in their objectives.

It is very common for an organization to be interested in many different areas of its network along with multiple potential attack paths. It is rare that a single hunt can cover all of those items and have room to spare. This is where prioritization and the likelihood of success come into play. As an example, let's say an organization cares about items A, B, and C. While item A is aligned with their top priorities, the resource cost to ensure the necessary coverage of that item is too much for the upcoming hunt. That item is shelved for another hunt, and instead, the focus is placed on items B and C for the hunters. In the event that item A is identified, the agreed-upon stakeholders could make an assessment to decide whether it meets their threshold of *bad*, or they could even use the word *severity*, in terms of that item. If this is found to be the case, they could adjust the hunt's priorities using the approved process and have the team pursue the new target to meet these evolving requirements.

But what if something else entirely comes up, for instance, a threat actor that was not even considered yet was found on the organization's enterprise? Well, the same process would be utilized. Always stick to the scope of the hunt while allowing the appropriate stakeholders to decide whether an adjustment needs to be made by the hunt team or have it passed off to another entity. Regardless of the path that is chosen, never forget the discussions in *Chapter 4, Communication Breakdown*. Do not assume, during planning or execution, that it is fine to ignore any new revelations from information that is found during the hunt. Assumptions such as this could be a major determent to the long-term success of an organization.

Assumptions

While not the most exciting portion of the planning, this is a very critical piece. If something fails in the development and communication of a plan, it will most likely be associated, in some way, with an assumption.

> **Definition**
>
> **Assumption**: An occurrence or finding that the team is planning on being either true or false.

Here are some common examples of assumptions that a team could list:

- The team will either have direct access to meaningful data from the target enterprise or will be provided with data by the customer.

- The team will be able to receive context for the data they analyze.

- The team will have adequate resources to complete the threat hunt within the allotted time.

With these assumptions, it is always a good practice to plan for them to be proven false. If the original plan was for a 5-member team to take 2 weeks for a particular hunt, then discuss and plan out what might happen if the team loses 2 individuals. This allows all the stakeholders to understand certain contingencies and confirm what is acceptable and what will cause the immediate failure of the hunt.

Success factors

This portion of planning is what separates the teams that *did things* and the ones that *did things that matter*. It is the simple act of outlining the requirements to include the tasks and objectives that will be measured against to quantify whether the hunt was a success.

A **measurement of performance** (**MOP**) attempts to determine the following: did the analyst perform the action correctly? If the action was to review network data between a certain period, then the MOP would ask the following question: did the analyst review the data in that period? MOPs have yes or no answers and are, typically, very straightforward in meaning with no wiggle room for interpretation. Each MOP is directly tied to a task, or a group of tasks, performed by the hunt analyst. Those tasks will always be directly linked to answering questions for one of the hypotheses. If this chain of logic is ever broken, this is a sign that the resources on the team are being wasted.

A **measurement of effectiveness** (**MOE**) attempts to determine the following: did the actions performed by the analyst have the intended effect that the team lead wanted to achieve? An example of an MOE would be based upon the completion of all outlined tactics to prove or disprove a hypothesis. If there was not enough data to effectively answer the hypothesis, then the MOE would be a failure. If there was enough data to effectively answer the hypothesis, then the MOE would be a success. There tends to be a lot of room for interpretation for MOEs due to the nature of a threat hunt. The team will need to use their best judgment and be objectively honest regarding the effectiveness of their hunt.

When outlining MOPs and MOEs, the question that will come up is do they all need to be successful or can some of them fail? It is up to each team to define the overall success criteria. It is very plausible to be unsuccessful in certain portions of a hunt and still remain successful overall. Each MOP and MOE will need to be annotated within the plan to state that it is either a critical item in order to be successful or one that is utilized to amplify success.

While it is nice to have a very well-thought-out plan in that changes will rarely need to occur, it very rarely happens that way. Adjustments, both planned and unplanned, will come up that the team will need to adjust to in order to overcome an unforeseen obstacle or meet an objective that did not pan out the way it expected. The flexibility to not crumble and, instead, adjust is built into the planning cycle in the form of planned deviations.

Planned triggers

This has already been hinted at in several areas; however, it can be very helpful to have a portion of hunt planning dedicated to it. It's important to plan for things to go wrong or that need to be changed. These events are also referred to as *triggers*. Some generic instances of when a trigger might occur and a change in threat hunter behavior would be necessary to remain on a successful hunt are listed as follows:

- Illegal activity is identified.

- An automated adversary is identified.

- An interactive adversary is identified.

Each of these areas would trigger the hunt analyst to change their standard behavior and process into a different cycle. The communication contracts and deviation plan will help the analyst, the team lead, and the customer to understand what will occur in these types of situations.

For example, if an analyst came across potential evidence of illegal activity, the agreed-upon deviation would be for the analyst to stop their analysis and immediately notify the team lead. The team lead would direct all hunt actions to cease on that portion of the enterprise. They would then contact all the predefined stakeholders. The customer would take over all of the defensive and investigative actions required on that portion of the enterprise.

Identifying the resources required

With everything identified in terms of what needs to be done, the team will then identify what is needed to make those plans a reality. During this portion of the planning session, the requirements concerning the technical construct of the team will need to be flushed out along with the physical needs regarding how the team will operate. While the following list is not all-inclusive, it can be used to build a picture of the questions that need to be answered in order to build a successful plan for the team:

- What are the knowledge requirements for the team? For example, the particular type of network (IT versus OT), Linux versus Windows, or an understanding of a particular coding or scripting language?

- Will dedicated individuals be required to maintain any equipment?

- Will there be unique language requirements, such as Spanish or Japanese, to facilitate communication with the host organization?

- What hardware-based resources will be required for the hunt? For example, network taps, switches, laptops, or servers for processing?

- What software-based resources will be required for the hunt? Any SIEMs, EDRs, or team collaboration tools?

- Will out-of-band communications for the team or the equipment need to be procured?

After outlining the technical and physical requirements along with how they will be fulfilled, it is time to start laying down some specific expectations for their use. Whether the team is on-site with the rest of the organization or spread across multiple geographical areas, the undying truth will remain that communication will make or break that mission. Formalizing communication pathways, tempos, and standard vernacular will be very beneficial when a mission is comprised of stakeholders with different backgrounds, cultures, and technical competencies.

Communication contracts

Creating a communication plan or contract is very simple but tends to be hard for inexperienced stakeholders to stick to. The contract begins with the identification of what the primary means of communication is, then the secondary means, and, if necessary, the tertiary means. This could mean stating that the first communication will occur via a specified chat program. If that fails, then via telephone, and if that fails, then via email.

Once the methods for communication are agreed upon, the means to communicate through those mediums will need to be established. If a chat program will be used, then where is that program? How do people gain access to it? Is there an expected schema for naming? Are there certain channels people will have access to? The same applies to telephone and email communications. The solution for outlining communication expectations does not have to be complicated or fancy.

The following example outlines a simple spreadsheet that was used to lay out the who, what, and where for each of the methods of communication:

Primary Communications Method			
	Rocket Chat - Channels	Members	
		Hunt Team	All
		Intel	Intel/Team Lead
		Request for Intel	All
		Analysts	Analysts/Team Lead
		Client Comms	Team Lead/Stakeholders
Seconday Communications			
	Email		
		Hunt Team - Subject: Hunt Team "TOPIC"	
		Request for Intel - Subject: RFI "TOPIC"	
		Analyst - Subject: As determined by the members	
		Client Comms - Subject: As determined by the Team Lead	
Tertiary Communications			
	Hunt team office phone - (213) 548-2296		
	Intel direct line - (554) 894-8852		
	Team lead direct line - (256) 847-2273		
	Stakeholder POC office line - (897) 894-5547		

Figure 7.1 – An example communications plan

This information will need to be treated as sensitive, and access to all communications channels must remain confidential to the team. The reason for this is that this is a view into the team's activities and their analyses of events in the enterprise. An intruder could use this information to help evade detection, or a well-meaning individual with a lack of full understanding could attempt to take action on discussions that occurred and cause havoc within the organization.

As the saying goes, *the best-laid plans of mice and men*. Outline your expectations, outline the requirements and what should happen, and document the plan. Once all of this is done, figure out how it can fail and then adjust to compensate. This is the topic of our next section, which is focused on stress testing plans and preparing for those things that should not happen.

Reviewing and stress testing the plan

Once the plan has been crafted, it is time to test it. The team will walk the plan step-by-step, identifying all the dependencies for each action. Trigger points for actions or deviations to happen will need to be formalized and documented as being either event-based or time-based. If those changes are event-based, identify the event. If they are time-based, identify what the time period is.

When conducting the review, flesh out the single points of failure and where the assumptions are hiding. Walk through the thought process in terms of what happens when unplanned events occur, and the plan fails. Is there a cascading failure? Does a single failure put undue strain on another area of the plan? This circular thought process should be embraced until, at a minimum, the tertiary impacts for events are identified and analyzed. Any impact that is deemed detrimental to the organization or hunt should have backup plans in place to minimize or reduce the risk or impact. The bigger the problem, the more sound the solution.

Real-World Example

During the planning of a 3-week threat hunt with a 10-member team, the team stress-tested their plan to identify potential secondary impacts. However, the team failed to identify what happens when the secondary impact compensations also failed. On that particular mission, the initial toolset used by all members failed to work. Shortly after, the secondary toolset was unable to be utilized as it did not fulfill the full requirements, which meant that only one person had access to the final toolset. The failure to fully stress test the plan led the team of 10 people to go from all members being able to execute actions to only 1 person being gainfully employed. This caused the forward movement to grind to a halt and almost caused the hunt to fail.

Normally, stress testing a plan is best led by an individual or group of individuals that are not too excitable and can keep the planning team in line. Plan for an analyst to be sick—sure. Plan for an alien invasion—probably not necessary. Do not get trapped by attempting to plan for *every* potential contingency. Identify those that are more likely to occur and be prepared to flex for the things that matter. In terms of those contingencies that appear to have a very low likelihood of occurring and a low impact on the hunt, communicate the impacts to all stakeholders, and move on with the mission.

Once this final piece is mapped out, tested, and the stakeholders feel as comfortable as they can, it is time to move onto the final phase. Receiving official approval for a well-documented and well-orchestrated plan is the best *official* communication method to ensure all stakeholders understand what will occur. In the next section, we will dive into this process and discuss some things to bear in mind.

Approving the plan

Once the plan is ready to execute, it must be approved. The approving panel should include feedback from all stakeholders, as it will be the last time to provide feedback and establish expectations prior to the hunt. The final approver will be the stakeholders who are granting the overall authorization for the hunt.

This plan approval will need to cover, at a minimum, the following:

- The stakeholders and the roles
- The restraints and the constraints
- The assumptions
- The team location and operating hours
- The scope (time and target systems)
- The deviation plan
- The communication contracts
- The trigger events
- The evidence of a stress test

With these items documented and formally approved by the appropriate stakeholders who can grant authorization for the hunt, the main planning phase is complete. The goal should always be to have a plan that is plainly documented and outlined so that a new stakeholder that arrives late to the hunt can pick up the plan and, within a short amount of time, understand everything that *should* happen.

Scenario A – internal threat hunt

The team lead starts planning for a threat hunt in Widget Makers Inc's networks. The initial restraints that the team identifies are listed as follows:

- Not impacting the non-intellectual property networks (for example, the commercial product networks).
- All illegal activity will be identified to the CEO and legal department lead only.
- The identification of an automated or interactive adversary will stop the hunt, and the FBI will be notified.
- There is no hunting on the operational technology networks.

Constraints communicated by the organization are listed as follows:

- The hunt will take no longer than 15 business days.

- A final written report will not be accomplished—it will be a verbal presentation only.

- Recommendations will be given to legal first to preserve attorney-client privilege.

- There is no direct communication between the threat hunt team, NOC, and SOC—everything goes through legal first.

Now the team moves to the scope, which the stakeholders confirm is only the intellectual property, government-connected networks, and supporting networks. This excludes at least 40% of the company, and the team lead lets the CEO know this is a rather large area to exclude for the hunt. The CEO is adamant about the scope, and the team lead makes sure the reason for scope constraint is in the planning document, clearly stating the network names to be excluded.

The team is provided with the network names, IP ranges, and connected network device hostnames to start the internal planning that has been vetted by legal.

Determining "bad" for the Widget Makers Inc threat hunt team is fairly straightforward, as they referenced the baseline indicators provided by the FBI form. The contract intel person has been able to add a few additional indicators to the list (for example, IPs, domains, malware hashes, or tactics employed by the threat actor) to provide additional specificity.

With the initial planning completed, the team takes a day to work through what they've identified and identify what assumptions they've got. First, this is accomplished by anonymous submissions via an *assumption box* that's available from the start of the planning. It is on this day that the box is opened, and each assumption is addressed by the full team. Afterward, brainstorming in a group is accomplished. Finally, all these assumptions are presented to the stakeholders to identify if there are ways to address them or if there is any way a stakeholder can provide clarity on the topic to reduce the scope of the assumption.

The following list is an example of the assumptions the team had that were addressed:

- Legal will provide updates to any questions within 2 hours (legal will prioritize this work during the hunt).

- Access to network devices will be unrestricted (granted).

- Access to government-connected networks will be unrestricted (denied, but legal will smooth the process).

- The team will be isolated during the hunt (confirmed).

Finally, the team turned to the success factors, MOPs, and MOEs. MOPs were defined by each section and supplied to the team lead for review. The team lead sent some back for further refinement and identified the development of separate MOPs they needed for a successful hunt. Some of these MOPs have been listed as follows:

- Analysts complete a review of the Windows event logs within 2 hours of receiving them.

- Intel supplies RFI responses within 6 hours of the request.

- The team lead provides responses to any inquiries within 15 minutes during normal operations.

- The network administrator acknowledges support requests within 5 minutes.

MOEs were determined by the team as well. The team lead then utilized these in a discussion with the stakeholders to ensure the internal team would be viewed as effective by the executives attached to the project. Some of the MOEs include the following:

- Identify the source of the beacons within 72 hours of starting the hunt.

- Clear intellectual property network of known campaign indicators.

- Identify known supply chain vulnerabilities in the intellectual property network within 10 days.

- Complete a targeted event log triage of the government-connected network within 15 days.

The internal team then stress tests the plan and works through any deviations, working through three steps of failure in the various activities they will accomplish throughout the hunt. The main deviations were identified when the restraints for the team were written.

Additional assumptions are identified, along with resource constraints. For example, if the workstations they're working on fail, there are laptops that are free to use, and the network administrator can configure them quickly. However, if those laptops die (due to a power outage or a natural disaster), there is no easy third step. The team lead takes these third-level failures to the stakeholders to identify a workaround that meets their requirements. In terms of the laptops, the CEO dedicates their offsite conference space, which will have live network access during the hunt in the case that the team has to displace.

Because of the organic nature of the team, there are a few additional resources from the outside that have not been covered in the initial planning. One of the main ones is a POC to work through for access to the government-connected network, which legal is working on. Additionally, there are some automated tools the team would like: EventLogExplorer, FTK Imager, and Axiom Forensics for each analyst workstation, which rises to $16,000. The CEO approves this cost after a discussion with the team lead about the impacts that not having this software would have.

Finally, the communication contracts are determined by the team lead in conjunction with the team and the stakeholders. You can see an example of their initial card presented earlier. However, the CEO refuses to get on Rocket.Chat, and wants all communications to be via email with the privileged header information at the top and Widget Maker Inc's lead counsel cc'd on every email. The lead counsel then asks the team lead to ensure there's a legal disclaimer banner on every chat channel. The team lead makes these changes.

The team lead presents the final plan to the stakeholders who are already very familiar with it since the communication was so open and direct. It is approved immediately with a start date within the month once the resources and personnel are ready.

Scenario B – external threat hunt

Since the team has been set, the team lead now works with the team to identify the restraints that the CSI personnel will utilize on this threat hunt. Some of the restraints that they determine are listed as follows:

- No hunting will take place on the operational network due to a lack of experience on CSI's part.
- Any legal findings will be handed off to the company immediately.
- Any automated or interactive adversary findings will immediately be identified to the company.
- All hunt and analysis work will be accomplished with strong chain-of-custody controls.

After the restraints are codified in the plan, the constraints are determined through meetings with stakeholders. Some of these constraints are listed as follows:

- Communication will remain within privileged channels for the organization.
- The threat hunt team will get all tools approved by the security team and legal department.

- All CSI personnel and subcontractors will be under an NDA for the threat hunt findings.

- The threat hunt will not take place on the finance network.

With the restraints and constraints codified into the plan, the team then turns to what the scope is for their new client. Some *no-go* areas have already been identified—the operational technology network and the finance network. The team lead working with the security team determines there are two additional networks that the team must remain away from, and provides names, IP ranges, and hostnames for the banned endpoints. Additionally, the security team provides information for the scope that is allowed, which is all other networks. This information is shared with the CSI team, but they aren't allowed to download it and work with it on their hunt network. Instead, the team lead must copy this information by hand to take to the team to be used in the development of the plan. This was dictated by legal counsel.

Then, the scope is added to the plan, listing the no-go networks and endpoints first, and the approved networks and endpoints for the hunt second. Through this planning phase, the security team lead states that network devices (such as routers and switches) are not to be directly accessed by the team. This is added to the constraints list.

Let's look at what *bad* means for this client; because the client has a security team, the finding of non-targeted attacks will be handed off to internal resources. Examples of non-targeted attacks include botnets not targeting critical information or infrastructure, generic malware without connection to the ongoing effects, phishing attempts, and more. Also, for this list, we can include that any malware, or suspicious data, that cannot be correlated within 4 hours to the greater impacts will be handed over to the security team. This allows the team to focus on activities and effects that are targeting what the executive team is most concerned about.

Next, the team starts to work on the assumptions of this plan. Some are easy to identify already—the threat actors are in the operational network—which CSI can't hunt on! CSI uses a whiteboard to start gathering assumptions at the start of planning. This list is kept up at all times to guide planning, address the assumptions, and allow the recording of new ones. Once the *assumption day* is reached on the calendar, the team gets together to brainstorm other assumptions over pizza. CSI's manner of doing this is direct. They use a method that they call *1 list, 2 challenges*. This is where someone lists an assumption but has to survive two challenges from peers to make sure the assumption isn't mundane and is applicable to the context of the hunt.

This list of assumptions is then presented to the stakeholders to attempt to address some of them and others that the stakeholders can identify. Some of the final assumptions are listed as follows:

- The team will be able to review data within 4 hours.
- The team will have access to network device information in 4 hours.
- The team will have internet access during the hunt for research purposes.

The success factors are determined after the assumptions have been worked through. For CSI, the MOP and the MOE are similar to the ones they've utilized in the past. This allows for some speed in this section of planning since the MOPs and MOEs only need to be tailored to the client environment. For the performance of actions, MOPs remain the same across clients. For example, consider the following:

- 4 hours for an analyst to review, tag, and process data through to the next handoff.
- Intel response to RFI's within 5 hours.
- Team leads provide a response to a request within 15 minutes.
- An example of tailored client MOPs
- Software library reviews are completed within 2 hours of acquisition.
- A network device log review within 3 hours of receiving them from the security team.

MOEs for the client are heavily dependent on the environment CSI's team is operating in. They are based on the hypotheses the team develops. Some of the MOEs for this threat hunt are listed as follows:

- A complete review of all network device firmware within 3 days.
- Identify all non-conforming software libraries and their anomalous code within 5 days.
- Clear the OT control network of malicious code.

Planned deviations have been discussed through this entire planning process with the stakeholders. Planning should never be done in isolation, and the CSI team's attempt to excel at communications with the clients during planning, to ensure the *warm and fuzzy* feeling of trust and partnership, grows from the beginning of the engagement. One deviation not previously discussed is an insider stealing data or causing malicious activities. Any evidence of this is to be isolated from the other forensics data, and the team lead will personally deliver it to the legal department.

Technical resources are all provided by the CSI team. Only physical space, network access, and accounts are needed by the team.

The communication contract mentioned previously is the same one that the team will be using. The only difference is for the aforementioned deviations, which are kept away from all planning documents.

The plan is then stress-tested and table-topped with the stakeholders to attempt to identify any weaknesses. The first one identified is a lack of access to the Intel individuals. An additional communication line, such as a direct cell phone, is added to the communications plan. Another area identified in the stress test is the inability to provide network device data within the time period planned due to an upgrade the security team has had scheduled. An elevation matrix is developed to prioritize work and is agreed to among the stakeholders. Additionally, more funds are put aside if the delay is caused by the client allowing the CSI team to complete the organizational goals.

The plan is then approved for execution!

Summary

A restraint is something the team does not want to occur. A constraint is something an external entity does not want to occur. The expected scope is required to be defined early on in the planning, as this sets the expectation of the who, what, where, and when of the threat hunt. Assumptions are everywhere in the plan and ignored by most. You need to specify what an assumption is in order to enhance the communication between the customer and the team.

MOPs are the yes or no answer to whether or not an analyst task was performed. MOEs are the answers to whether the group of tasks performed by the analyst had the intended effect. MOPs and MOEs allow the team to articulate their level of effectiveness against the hypotheses throughout the hunt.

Ensure that you identify the requirements the team needs to successfully execute the threat hunt. Any limitations need to be identified and remediated ahead of execution of the hunt. Deviations occur, so plan for them as best as you can. If nothing else, outline the process to acknowledge and approve deviations.

Stress test the plan and identify secondary and tertiary impacts due to failures. Any failure to do so will increase the risk taken on by the team throughout the hunt and could cause the hunt to fail.

With the plan formalized, it will be time to begin execution. Prior to this, the team will need to understand what their primary goal throughout the threat hunt is. It is not to find the adversary; it is to ensure protection from the adversary. They will need to protect the customer's data, the customer's enterprise from further exploitation, and protect themselves as they have just, potentially, become a target. In the next chapter, we will cover these three areas, including considerations for each item, along with ways to mitigate or reduce risks that the team will be taking on through the life cycle of the hunt.

Review questions

Answer the following questions to check your knowledge of this chapter:

1. A _____ is an action or event that the team does not want to occur.
    A _____ is an action or event that an external entity does not want to occur.

2. Ineffective _____ could lead to a hunt team believing that they should be looking for one thing, while the organization believes that they are looking for something else.

3. Once a scope has been approved for a hunt, can it be modified?

4. An _____ is an occurrence or finding that the team or organization is planning on, but not confirming, being either true or false.

5. Why should a team stress test a plan?

Review answers

The answers to the review questions are as follows:

1. Restraint; constraint.

2. Communication.

3. Yes, only by the preapproved stakeholders.

4. Assumption.

5. To identify what happens when unplanned events occur and the plan fails, then provide solutions for anything that cannot be tolerated.

Part 2: Execution – Conducting a Hunt

Here, you will gain an understanding of how to execute a threat hunt and what to consider during this phase.

This part of the book comprises the following chapters:

- *Chapter 8, Defending the Defenders*
- *Chapter 9, Hardware and Toolsets*
- *Chapter 10, Data Analysis*
- *Chapter 11, Documentation*

8
Defending the Defenders

Now that all of the planning is done, it is a great time to remind everyone on the threat hunting team why they are there. At the most basic level, the goal of the team is to negatively impact a threat actor's day by disrupting, impeding, or completely negating their activities and potentially preventing the *bad guys* from achieving their long-term goals. This could mean impacting those threat actors with millions in lost revenue by removing accesses that could have taken years to establish or blocking the phishing email lures that were just discovered. With a hunt, you could find legacy threats that are still valid or a new threat.

At a minimum, the data the team will be accessing and recording must be protected as much as possible. A legal phrase for this situation is ensuring the threat hunt team is executing their *due diligence*. A simple way to evaluate the data storage requirements for a threat hunt is that it's bad if the customer has a vulnerability and loses data, however, the team should never be the source of that vulnerability or data leak. The threat hunt team should never introduce more vulnerabilities to the organization. Additionally, depending upon the adversaries that are targeting the organization, the hunters themselves could be put into a position where their equipment and physical safety could be at risk.

In this chapter, we are going to cover the following topics:

- Protecting the data
- Protecting the team's equipment
- Protecting the team
- Scenario A—internal threat hunt
- Scenario B—external threat hunt

By the end of the chapter, you will be able to do the following:

- *Comprehend* the importance of protecting organizational data.
- *Comprehend* the importance of protecting hunting equipment.
- *Identify* the importance of protecting team members.

Protecting the data

The importance of protecting the customer's data cannot be understated – as soon as the team accesses customer data or their network, the team has the primary responsibility of protecting that access. Data protection is the team's main goal and comes before any of the other requirements within the threat hunting plan. Failure to do so is not just a failure of the hunt but of the threat hunting team.

During planning, the network and data types that will be reviewed will have been identified along with the customer organization's expectations and requirements for the protection of that data. For example, if the team will be accessing a network that has **Payment Card Information** (**PCI**) data on it and the team will be viewing that data, then they must comply with the same cybersecurity standards as the original organization. The easiest way to know what data requires specific security requirements is to ask the organization during the scoping in the planning process.

If at any point in time there are certain levels of protection or data sensitivity that the team is unsure about, they must ask the organization upon realizing the data might require enhanced security. It is much simpler to identify ahead of time that the team is not a fit for a particular part of the hunt than to assume it won't be an issue. If the assumption is made and the team goes through with the hunt, it will cause a bigger issue, potentially threatening the entire hunt and the team's employment/contract status. The saying *it is better to ask for forgiveness than it is for permission* does not apply here. Be honest and be upfront. A concern kept to the team could cost both the customer and the team money and resources to rectify.

A very simple way to protect data that can go overlooked is the use of encryption. Is data stored somewhere? Encrypt it. Is it being transmitted somewhere? Encrypt it. Unless it is actively being reviewed by an analyst then it should always be encrypted.

While the concept of *chain of custody* typically is not included in a threat hunt, the team should always be able to identify where data is stored and minimize any possibility of that data leaving the team's control.

Here are some tips for protecting data:

- Encrypt all data stored at rest.

- Encrypt all transmissions between systems: from the client to the hunt team and hunt team members.

- Minimize, control, and account for all removable media that comes into the vicinity of the hunt team's equipment.

- Control the hunt team's operating environment by not allowing non-trusted members inside or near the equipment.

When protecting data, there are two main types of level of protection required. The first type of protection is for data that should *never* be released and those types of datasets that should be protected for a set amount of time. While there is a fine difference between how the data will be protected, understand that there can be a difference between the types of data. Items such as a company's trade secrets are something that should be protected for an indefinite time. The details about the *where* and *when* of an upcoming threat hunt are an example of something that should be protected at least until the hunt is over, so as not to potentially tip off an adversary about the upcoming event. As such, planning an upcoming hunt on a team's private chat channel might be alright but transferring the customer's data through the same medium would not be. This brings us to the next section, on considerations for protecting the team's equipment.

Protecting the team's equipment

Protecting the team's hardware can range from defending against the innocent passerby that accidentally turns off equipment to the malicious insider that is actively attempting to sabotage the threat hunt. As previously mentioned, having a secure *war room* is the first step to enabling this protection. This place could be a hotel room or conference area that only the team has access to.

Some potential requirements to take into consideration for this area are the following:

- Secure access limited to the threat hunting team and cleared personnel

- Ability to prevent cleaning crews and other third-party entities from entering the space

- After-hours security if not operating 24/7 throughout the hunt

- Adequate bandwidth to the network

- Adequate and secure bandwidth for open source research

- Ample power for all equipment

- Ample cooling for all equipment and personnel

Understand that a location being selected as a *secure location* just means that it is more secure than other areas. Most of the time, it is impractical to fully secure any area unless the threat hunt is conducted around the clock. During these off-hours, the team will need a method that will help to secure all equipment and protect it from tampering. If tampering does occur, then the team will want to know about it. Simple items such as portable surveillance cameras and tamper-proof locks can assist with this. Utilizing items like these can, in even the worst-case scenario, let the team know that their secure area has been breached and that they should react accordingly.

How far a team goes with the concept of work-area protection and security needs to be weighed appropriately against the cost of implementing measures. Who is the team willing and capable of protecting against? The protection against more advanced adversaries requires the overall cost of protection to increase. A large pelican case with a heavy-duty lock can help reduce the chance of theft due to opportunity, however, it would not stop a nation-state adversary from accessing the equipment overnight and modifying the hardware. Oftentimes just knowing that someone was tampering with the hunt team's equipment may be enough protection. This in turn would allow the team to acquire new equipment and adjust their tactics to respond to the physical intrusion.

Protecting the team

"Just because you are paranoid doesn't mean people aren't out to get you."

Why would there be a section in a cyber threat hunting book that discusses personal protection? While the hunt itself is executed in a place that is made up entirely of the 1's and 0's of the electromagnetic spectrum, those doing the execution live in the physical domain. The physical domain has threats that encryption will not address; for certain adversaries, the simplest way to ensure success is to remove the opportunity for a defender to defend the enterprise. This could be through physical manipulation, theft, or even violence. Will this be the case for the majority of hunt operations that teams undertake? No. Physical interaction with adversaries is possible when dealing with an inside threat or when the adversary is of the higher tiers, such as organized crime or nation-state actors.

A threat hunt can put teams into very interesting positions where their main goal, unknown to the team, is to stop an adversary that stands to make a large sum of money if the intrusion is successful. What if the adversary feels that their life or those that they care about is in the balance if they fail at an intrusion? Some individuals or organizations might have more riding on that particular intrusion than the entire team has risked. These are just a few of the interpersonal drivers that are buried deep under the bytes that are sifted through during a hunt.

No matter how minor or insignificant a particular hunt may feel to the team, they need to understand that they are only a small piece of the puzzle. The adversary has a very large say in how quickly and far actions progress. Hotels can be broken into, staff can be paid off to perform certain actions. It might not be resource-intensive to follow individuals throughout their day. The entire team should go into the hunt with *eyes open* on who the potential adversaries are that they might go up against. This mindset becomes more and more of a factor for a select group of hunt missions that start to cross geographic boundaries. Hunts, and threat hunt teams, that cross national boundaries are more likely to become involved in matters of national interest. Any hunt that centers around items or concepts of national interest will have literally unlimited resources available provided by the impacted nation to impede threat hunters.

What does this even mean for a team? Would performing a threat hunt remotely for a company imply that the team will be targeted by an adversary and monitored all of the time? Not likely. As stated previously, this level of response from an adversary is not something that will apply to all hunters. However, if you are part of an on-site hunt that is operating in a country where a sudden offer of $200 USD could change an individual's life, then the risk factor would be increased. If the adversary that you are impacting is sophisticated enough, they could readily have resources available in the same area to apply pressure to a team. The sudden realization for an unsuspecting individual that they are being followed throughout the day and their hotel room has been searched could be enough to impact what they are willing to report in a debrief.

What can you and your team do to protect yourselves if it means that the adversary may be backed by an entire country's efforts? This will all depend on what the identified threat is and how much the team wants to proactively counter it. Some considerations that the team should take into consideration throughout the life cycle of the threat hunt are the following:

- Know the adversary – who might you encounter, what are their capabilities, and could they be local to the team during the hunt?

- Push back on any public notification of the hunt until after it is completed.

- Set the stage for the team to minimize unnecessary communication throughout the hunt.

- No social media posts.

- No references should be made in public about any upcoming activity or trips.

- Use burner phones while traveling – no personal devices are allowed.

- Always travel in pairs, never by yourself – ever.

- No mind-altering substances – this includes alcohol.

- Be courteous, not friendly with individuals.

- Have prepared responses for standard questions such as *who are you and what are you doing here?*.

- Be mindful of and prepared to react to things that *do not feel right.*

New equipment can be purchased, but a life taken cannot be restored. Always protect yourself and those in your team. Does this mean that you should try to protect your team from an entire nation at every turn? No. Scope the threat hunt and the hunt team's internal defenses against the intended adversary. If the team is intended to hunt for the equivalent of a *smash and grab* cyber adversary whose target is one of opportunity and not targeting, the team probably does not need to put on their tinfoil hats just yet. However, if the adversary they are combating is of the higher tiers, the team's defenses should be prepared to extend beyond what the adversary is willing to employ.

Scenario A – internal threat hunt

The team has a prepared location inside the facility to execute the hunt operations from. Network access has been confirmed, as well as power and cooling. The team already has a plan to use SSH to connect to the devices they need to for data gathering and review. As the hunt team does not have the ability to operate out-of-band and must rely on the existing infrastructure to retrieve data from their new sensors, encryption between the devices is a must. The network administrator has used their access to the NOC to get some servers and standalone storage for the team. The equipment set up by the network administrator has data at rest policies applied to it upon writing to disk.

Before starting, the team lead verifies with the SOC and NOC about any of the current collection locations requiring additional security. Legal has negotiated access to the government-connected networks. However, the data stored there must be physically separate from the data stored for the organization. The network administrator works with the organization to get an additional server and portable hard drive to move data to once gathered by analysts.

Additional procedures are put in place for the analysts to use when gathering the data from the government-connected networks and endpoints. The team lead also sets new expectations with the stakeholders for the analysis of the government-connected data. Since the security requirements are higher and the data cannot be accessed via the threat hunt network enclave, this specific data will be reviewed in batches every few days. This allows time for pre- and post-sanitization of the environment. Also, the hunt will now need to take a longer period than originally agreed to. The stakeholders agree to these concerns.

The threat hunter's war room is set up with locks only the team and facility manager have access to. The team lead meets with the facility manager, their supervisor, and a senior-vice president stakeholder to ensure the importance of denying access to un-approved visitors is clear. The team lead follows this meeting up with an email covering what was discussed also.

The threat to the equipment is assessed as low since they're employees of the same organization they're hunting and have not yet had any concerns expressed to or about them. The team decides to only lock the war room doors and put up two remote cameras that record the door exterior and cover most of the interior of the war room area. The video is saved to a cloud application.

The team also assesses the threat to each member physically as low due to the same reasons. The team lead does ask the members to be aware of probing questions, even from friends and co-workers. The need for privacy in the war room is reiterated and also that visitors are not allowed. Any infractions of the personal and physical security of the space could be met with termination of employment.

Before the first scheduled day of the hunt, the team comes in and thinks that some of the papers and whiteboard have been moved. They review the camera footage, and someone entered the war room in the early morning and took pictures of the entire war room. One laptop is picked up and moved to where the camera doesn't cover but is put back. The team lead immediately informs the stakeholders and goes about quickly assessing if there's been a compromise of the laptop. After a quick and inconclusive check, the laptop and footage are handed over to the organization's security team. This is in line with the restraints and constraints of the threat hunt.

Scenario B – external threat hunt

The CSI team begins to set up the war room on-site in the space that the organization set aside. The small conference room has good connectivity, cooling, and even windows! It is also in an area that has low foot traffic and is monitored by the on-site security team via cameras and alarms 24/7. The team lead has a meeting with the security team and a vice president level stakeholder to make sure the expectations for the security of the war room are well understood. They follow the meeting up with an email documenting the conversation.

The room itself is accessible via a card reader and pin. The hunt team is set up with access and starts moving into the space. The team brings in their own equipment to set up in the new war room. All laptops are locked to the desks. All equipment has tracking devices secured to them (for example, tile trackers). There are three additional remote cameras that are installed, giving full coverage of the war room. The servers the team is going to use are in heavy-duty pelican cases weighing over 120 lbs. These cases are secured to pillars in the room that are holding up the ceiling.

The CSI team has processes and procedures already in place dealing with data storage and data transmission security. The team will be accessing the client networks through a VPN connection that will be set up to cut the connection if the VPN fails. Additionally, each workstation will be connecting to network endpoints via SSH or HTTPS for devices accessible via a web frontend. Data at rest is encrypted upon a write to the disks in the data storage array. The team lead asked the client during planning if there were any protected networks that required additional security requirements. Due to some of the exclusions in scope, there are no networks the client would need additional security for.

The CSI team is not familiar with the area, or the individuals who work at the organization. They've attempted to keep a low profile during the hunt and are dressing the same as other employees. The CEO has supplied the whole team with company polos to assist in fitting in better. The team will also not use the on-site cafeteria and work slightly off-hours to reduce the chance of interactions with current employees.

The team lead doesn't feel that there's any concern from a nation-state actor in the current area. However, they are near an international airport and border. He tasks the intelligence contractor to see if there's any information targeting the organization or the threat hunt team. After a few days, the intelligence professional comes back with a little bit of light chatter about the organization, with no clear nation-state activity from the evidence found. The team lead asks for this check to be done every 3 days during the hunt to ensure there's no change to the team's risk profile.

The team lead reminds the rest of the team about the security procedures in a low-threat environment: ensure they're never alone outside the war room and their hotel rooms; be courteous but not friendly to individuals they meet; breakfast and dinner will be in the hotel restaurant to reduce the risk of exposure and temptations to drink. Any violations of this will impact their employment status and could impact the hunt itself.

Summary

The threat hunt team is there to counter an adversary. This countering extends beyond just the cyber domain. The team's top priority should always be to protect the data that they gather for the hunt. Encrypt transmissions and data storage, and maintain accountability for any portable devices that could have data on them. To protect the data, the team's equipment must also be strongly secured both logically and physically. Control the team's operating spaces as much as possible. When operating space security is limited, secure the equipment as much as is reasonably possible.

Above all else, the team members themselves are more valuable than any piece of data or equipment. Some adversaries have worked physical exploitation into their attack processes. Always protect yourselves and each other. Now that we have covered how to not become the vulnerability during a hunt, in the next chapter, we will take a closer look at some sample hardware and toolsets that are commonly employed on missions.

Review questions

Answer the following questions to check your knowledge of this chapter:

1. Encryption can be a very powerful control for a team in order to protect _____.

2. (True or False) Allowing unknown members into the hunt team's spaces is alright.

3. Could storing all of the hunt team's equipment in an unlocked closet present any problems? If so, what?

4. Would an adversary ever target a hunt team?

Review answers

The answers to the review questions are as follows:

1. Data

2. False

3. Yes, anyone with access could have the opportunity to steal or modify the equipment.

4. Yes

9
Hardware and Toolsets

In *Chapter 7, Planning*, the process of identifying resource requirements for the threat hunt was discussed. This chapter goes over the planning for resources in greater detail. The first item that the team must identify is the type of target networks and technologies that they will be interfacing with. This determination will aid them in identifying the personnel and equipment required to conduct the hunt.

Every hunt can and should be customized to the target network. This could include going so far as to establish a dedicated private cloud that a sensor can use a VPN to connect through for the team to be able to export outside the organization's, or a possible threat actor's, direct observation. While this book is not intended to be a technical how-to book, we will cover the higher-level capabilities that a team will need to have at the ready for the hunt.

Regardless of the target network's physical location or whether it is an **information technology (IT)**-based or **operational technology (OT)**-based network, the team should always plan to do the same thing an adversary does and attempt to live off the land. To say this another way, the team should *use the tools that are already available*. There is normally a massive amount of data and administrative tools available to hunt teams that already exist on the target network. This does not mean that the team should never deploy any equipment or software on the enterprise, but rather that the team should have the mindset of starting with what is already there and slowly building up from that.

Why does this matter? Because an adversary seeing a new piece of software called **EnCase** that is not designed for day-to-day administration being installed on a system will send a message (see *Chapter 4, Communication Breakdown*, for more on communication). It is easy to search through security articles on the internet and find stories of woe concerning adversaries that responded in a dramatic fashion once they perceived that someone was after them. Unless the team is intending to act dramatically and make a statement, build from the ground up and default to using what is already there.

In this chapter, we are going to cover the following topics:

- Hunting on IT networks versus OT networks versus cloud networks
- Questions that drive requirements
- In-band versus out-of-band
- Hardware
- Software tools
- Scenario A—internal threat hunt
- Scenario B—external threat hunt

By the end of the chapter, you will be able to do the following:

- *Comprehend* the different approaches needed when conducting a hunt on an IT network, OT network, or cloud network.
- *Discuss* the difference between in-band and out-of-band communication.
- *Identify* the different types of hardware and software that could be employed.

Hunting on IT networks versus OT networks versus cloud networks

IT networks and OT networks are fundamentally similar. They are so similar, in fact, that it is easy to mistake a common action that is permitted on IT networks, such as port scanning, as being fine on an OT network and ending up bringing operations to a halt. If this is the first time you are hearing about this difference, the only thing that you need to take away is to stay off OT networks until you can learn about them in depth, with lots of training in a segregated training environment.

The vast majority of personnel in cybersecurity have built their entire careers on IT networks. The software they use, tactics, and experiences are all centered around what is *normal* on systems. Reactions to finding non-standard software or connections, such as *a bot that is connected to a command-and-control server is bad and should be removed immediately*, are very common. However, on an OT network, these ideas and concepts do not always translate. Why? Isn't malware bad? Yes, it is, but the main purpose of an OT network is to facilitate operations. Is the malware impacting operations? No. Will removing the malware impact operations? Yes. So, you cannot remove it, but can you isolate the system so that it cannot spread or contain it another way? While not the most attractive solution, sometimes a system owner's only course of action will be to ensure that remediation of the system will be incorporated into the next scheduled downtime, which could be years away. Until then, the local cyber defenders would need to monitor that system in order to ensure that the malicious incursion does not spread.

While this is a very specific example, the differences quickly become evident the more an analyst dives into OT environments. The blanket recommendation is that if a hunt team is required to hunt on an OT and IT environment, the OT portion of the team should be dedicated to that task and staffed with individuals experienced in those styles of networks. Mixing during the hunt is a *very bad idea* due to the differences, possible confusion, and impacts on an operational environment.

Cloud environments bring in another potential discussion point for the team as they can limit certain response types. First off, it can be extremely complicated or hard to put a tap between systems within a cloud environment. Secondly, depending upon the cloud account types, services utilized, or auditing enabled, certain styles of hunting might be beyond the scope of the organization to even allow. If the organization's cloud service is a **Software as a Service** (**SaaS**) type, due to the nature of the service, they have inherently outsourced the risk of the service's underlying operating system and hardware to the cloud provider. At most, the team will be able to assist in validating software-level behavior.

Hybrid environments are becoming more and more common, with enterprises becoming less and less defined by the physical boundaries of an organizational building. This means countless enclaves within a larger enterprise, each with its own baseline, requirements, and authorization authority.

Questions that drive requirements

There are several questions that help narrow down or open up hardware requirements:

- Will the network owner provide equipment, or will the team use their own?

- Is the team allowed to bring their own equipment?

- Will the team be allowed to return with their equipment, or will it have to stay behind?

- Are there any space, power, cooling, noise, or transportation limitations? When transporting equipment, it needs to arrive *and* work:

  - Just because a box technically meets United States airline requirements, it does not mean that the equipment inside will be fully functioning. Even cases that are designed to be rugged and hold sensitive equipment can be opened and their contents adjusted.

  - Each country has its own unique flying requirements, some with much smaller checked baggage allowances than others. If flying between multiple airlines, ensure that *all* of the aircraft can handle the bags your team brings.

- Where will the team operate both physically and logically?

  - Will they be on-site with the network administrators? Will the team be split with some on-site and some back at their home office?

  - Will the team's equipment be allowed to have its own out-of-band connection?

> **Real-World Example**
>
> During a hunt mission, a team had to take a few cases of equipment, including servers, on an airline flight. All bags met the travel requirements and had all the proper documentation. When those cases were picked up at the end of the flight, it was obvious that they had been tampered with.
>
> All of the equipment had been physically removed along with the hard drives. Afterward, they were haphazardly placed back in. Needless to say, none of the equipment worked after that. Even if it did, the team would have been very hesitant to use anything that was physically dismantled in flight.

While a hunt mission might perform better with several pieces of equipment, it is not always feasible to bring them. Being able to think outside of the normal paradigms will greatly help. While bringing a few large switches would be best, can the team make do with smaller pocket switches that are easier to transport? Can equipment be purchased locally? Just because there is one way the team *normally* operates does not mean that is how they will always be able to. A perfect example of such a case is how a hunt teams' equipment is deployed and they receive data. Do they completely isolate themselves from the target network, or is there a connection between their systems and where they are hunting? In the next section, we will cover the ups and downs of each approach for how a team's systems communicate with each other.

In-band versus out-of-band

An in-band connection for a threat hunting team means that the threat hunters' equipment will be connected directly to the target network. All communication traverses the same network that they are hunting on. A threat hunter will be able to sit at their workstation and remotely connect to an endpoint (for example, a server) to download logs or do live hunting. The pro and con of this type of connection are as follows:

- *Pro*: Extremely easy to establish with the least amount of effort.

- *Con*: Extremely noisy to the adversary; any attempt to measure the *baseline* activity of the target network will be different from how it truly looks as it will not include traffic and activity from the threat hunt team.

An out-of-band connection means that only a limited number of *listening* devices will be connected to the physical target network. All other equipment and communication will take place on a network isolated from the target. A threat hunter will need to have endpoint logs, either gathered by the devices or the administrators of the network and loaded into the threat hunt tooling. The pro and con of this type of connection are as follows:

- *Pro*: Much harder for an adversary to detect, which minimizes hunt analyst activity impacting the target network

- *Con*: Harder to establish, requiring additional equipment and time for activities

Whenever possible, use out-of-band connections for all equipment and communication with anyone on the team or target organization. This adds an additional layer of security and separation between a perceived adversary and the defenders. Threat hunters normally do not have the luxury of hunting for as long as they like. Adversaries, on the other hand, tend to have the ability to go completely quiet for 6 months to a year in order to wait out a loud defender.

These two different methods of managing data pathways can drastically impact the requirements for the mission. If there is in-band communication, there might be a lower requirement for infrastructure-style devices. If there is out-of-band communication, equipment dedicated to providing a remote reach-back capability could be necessary. In the next section, we will go over examples of these various pieces of equipment and their uses.

Hardware

In this section, we will list some standard equipment that can be utilized and its intended purpose. Always customize the threat hunt to the unique requirements of the network and team. We will start out with perimeter defense technologies and quickly move onto various pieces of infrastructure that can be utilized throughout a hunt mission.

Perimeter defense

Equipment that performs this type of function will be your hunt team's first line of defense between your systems and any external systems. In all but some of the more extreme isolation hunts, there will be a level of connectivity between the systems used for hunting and external systems. A few things to consider and understand when establishing this *secure* enclave are as follows:

- There is normally a dedicated security device between the out-of-band hunt network and the customer's network and internet.

- Prior to installation, have a team member perform a vulnerability scan of the defensive system from the external side of the device. This will allow the team to better understand how the device appears to an outsider and how it could be perceived by an outside entity. Something simple, such as if an attempted remote connection to the system returns a blank cursor, could be very telling. If the device returns a banner page, then substantial information could be conveyed to an adversary to include that a new device is now present that does not match the surrounding network.

- Multiple methods depending upon the level of security needed – a router with a strict **access control list** (**ACL**), or full prevention systems that would target specific traffic based on behaviors or signatures.

If the team is required to operate in a completely isolated fashion, then infrastructure such as this might not be necessary. However, transferring data and coordinating with external parties could prove to become a cumbersome activity. Bringing some of those communication gaps brings us to the next common piece of equipment used during hunting missions: routers.

Routers

These types of devices are the foundation of the internet, as they handle large traffic volumes with grace. There is a universe of several types and styles of routers out there, each with its own pros and cons. The following are some high-level insights to keep in mind when identifying whether routers should be included in the team's equipment list:

- Layer 3 device (ref: OSI Model).

- Forwards data between computer networks and performs traffic-directing functions on the internet.

- If planning on deploying infrastructure onto the target network, always match the style and versioning of equipment already present. If the target network only uses a very specific type of switch, use the same one. This will prevent potential compatibility issues as well as preventing the team from standing out to anyone that is monitoring for *new* devices.

It is good to understand that routers are not the only piece of infrastructure equipment that could be required as there are a few more layers to the OSI Model that traffic is moved across. Stepping down one rung on the OSI ladder will bring us to the next item of interest: switches.

Switches

If you go back a decade or two, switches and routers had a large chasm between them. In today's world, they are utilized *almost* interchangeably. Please note that there is a difference in some of their capabilities and what they can do:

- Layer 2 device (ref: OSI Model).

- If you have a Layer 3 switch, it has visibility into both Layer 2 and Layer 3 protocols; however, it will typically just lack the WAN port found on routers.

- If planning on deploying infrastructure onto the target network, match the style of equipment already present. Doing so could cause a service interruption on the target network.

Comparing routers and switches, many devices on the market blend the two and offer the capabilities of both. However, by definition, a router is focused on Layer 3 traffic (packets), and switches will be more focused on Layer 2 traffic (frames). Each layer has its own indicators that can be observed of adversarial behavior. In certain instances, there might be earlier ways to observe live network data.

TAPs versus SPANs

If there is not a default location to obtain network traffic, two methods exist in order to see what is traveling across the *wires* that make up networks. These methods can *easily* allow a team to gain near-real-time insight into traffic as it is moving on the network, something that is not always possible by reviewing logs of other systems. The following is a breakdown of some common differences between employing a TAP on a network compared to utilizing SPANs:

- Installing TAPs is one of the best ways to ensure you can receive all data from a network connection. When it comes to hiding in plain sight from an adversary, TAPs cannot be beaten. A breakdown of the general insights for this type of equipment are as follows:

  - An adversary will not be able to *see* you, as a TAP is a *dumb* device that simply forwards on traffic.

  - Requires some downtime to install devices and get traffic re-started.

  - Can be expensive.

  - Must check that the TAP can keep up with the line that it is bisecting.

  - Typically, does not have any concerns with network speeds. As long as the TAP is rated for the line it is listening to, it will be able to capture all of the traffic.

- The alternative to TAPs is a **Switched Port Analyzer** (**SPAN**) port on the target infrastructure. This method is just as common to employ as TAPs, but flip the pros and cons to the other side. A breakdown of the general insights for this type of equipment are as follows:

  - A SPAN is visible to anyone that is logged into the networking device and reviewing the configuration. What type of adversary is the team hunting or concerned with?

  - Not all ports are created equal; ensure you have adequate bandwidth.

  - Depending upon the size of the SPAN, it can cause issues with the infrastructure device performance.

  - A SPAN can cause strain on the networking device and should be monitored by administrators to ensure no operational impact.

  - It does not inherently cause a service interruption (see the preceding point) and is normally the easiest to get approved by leadership.

Reviewing traffic logs from infrastructure devices and other monitors can be very beneficial. Unfortunately, there are ways to misinterpret those items, or even for an adversary to trick them into not reporting certain events. When it comes to monitoring active network traffic, the communication *must* occur and there is no method of hiding that it did. An adversary can encrypt it, split it, or obfuscate it in a dozen different ways; however, it will happen, and it can be captured using these items. This brings us to our next topic: discussing what is needed to perform that collection.

Data collection sensors

The equipment that performs this type of function often proves to be some of the most valuable pieces of equipment during a hunt mission. While being very important, they also can be easy to misjudge the requirements that can be causing problems when analyzing data. Can the sensor keep up with the flow of data it is monitoring? Does the sensor put the results in a proprietary format that the team cannot understand? The following are a few things to consider when deciding whether and how data collection sensors are needed:

- Chances are the network owner will not have on hand all the required sensors you need to conduct the hunt. In this case, the team will need to deploy some of their own.

- Always place the sensor as close to the source of interest as possible. Placing the sensor too far away from a target will allow it to capture extraneous traffic. However, placing it too close may cause the team to not see the whole conversation between multiple systems.

- Identify any overlap in sensors and duplication of logs along with plans to remediate the issue. Aggregation of events becomes nearly impossible when a single packet is picked up by three sensors and each reports them as a separate occurrence.

- Some considerations for the sensor(s) are as follows:

  - Will the sensor stream data back to the hunt network or be manually retrieved?

  - Will the sensor conduct any filtering before it returns data?

  - How much buffer (storage) space will be required?

  - Will the sensor be left after the mission, or will it be retrieved?

  - Is there a concern about someone tampering with the sensor?

At this point in the review of equipment, the team will have a lot of source points for collecting information. The next stage will be to review where to place all of this information, in either short-term or long-term storage.

Centralized storage

Storage comes in many different styles with varying read/write speeds, accessibility, and longevity of the data itself. Some mediums are very temporary but extremely fast to access. Others might be a little slower but could easily be stored, in the correct conditions, for years. The following are a few things to consider when identifying storage requirements:

- Is there a need for a dedicated device or system for the storage of data of interest?

- Determine the team's data gathering purposes before deciding on size requirements – a team taking an output-driven mindset and only storing what is needed versus an input-driven mindset and collecting everything and then filtering it later.

- Take into consideration the physical security of data and fault tolerance.

- The retention period and controls can also play a major factor in the type and amount of storage; always check whether there are local regulations that dictate any specific controls that must be in place.

- For a small team operating out-of-band of the target network, network-attached storage with several TBs of space is typically sufficient for a short hunt.

- The top priority of any hunt is to ensure protection from disclosure or loss of any customer data that the team retrieves from the network. The intent is to aid and improve security, not become the vulnerability.

With the storage of data done, the team will have another consideration to make. Will they need direct access to anything on the network that is being hunted on? If so, how will they access those items? This is where the concept of jump boxes comes into play.

Jump boxes

What makes a jump box special? Is there a particular sensor installed or specialized software? There can be, but it is not required. This type of system is a designated system, or systems, that the hunters will use to pivot through the network. You can think of it as a controlled entry point into a hostile environment. The following list highlights a few things to understand about the concepts behind using a jump box:

- It limits all interaction between the hunt team and the target network to a handful of systems.

- Those systems should be closely monitored by defenders for any activity that occurs to, or on, them.

- Systems should be in the same IP space as the network system administrators, assuming the team wants to blend in.

- Accounts used on the system should be of the same convention as the network system administrators, assuming the team wants to blend in.

- Be sure to remove the accounts when the hunt is over!

Regardless of whether the team decides they will need these types of systems on a hunt, they will need offline systems of their own that never directly touch the target network. This brings us to the next group of equipment to consider.

Systems to analyze data

Each hunt team can have a unique take on how they decide to analyze data. This might be through the employment of very powerful laptops that they carry around with them. Others might choose to utilize cloud computing. Some teams might have powerful systems in their home offices away from the hunt that can be utilized for this function:

- Laptops are great to use for portability in unusual terrain, as processing power can be low compared to other solutions. The hunt team could dedicate a few systems for processing larger datasets if a server or off-premises analysis is not available.

- Cloud storage and analysis can be extremely versatile and inexpensive to utilize. The biggest hurdle will be managing the legalities and approval to transfer customer data off-site and into the appropriate cloud provider.

- Dedicated servers are the team's home away from home. The team can maximize computing power, memory, and storage in a very repeatable way. The downsides are they are typically heavy and bulky. Also, a larger footprint like this will normally require someone on-site dedicated to managing those devices.

At this point, we have covered the key pieces of equipment needed; while not an all-inclusive list, it will get the bigger items accounted for. Next, we will discuss the pieces of software that can be employed throughout the hunt on the systems mentioned previously.

Software tools

When choosing software to utilize, there are a few things that the team will need to take into consideration:

- Team experience with toolsets for both using them and maintaining them.

- Existing capabilities inherit on the target network.

- Authorization to deploy new capabilities on the target network.

- Any known vulnerability or alternate uses of the toolset. Ensure that nothing being employed by the team or deployed on the network can be utilized by an adversary to their advantage.

- The perception intended to present to an adversary. Tanium showing up might not come across as defensive as it has a wide range of uses by maintenance, but a Carbon Black agent would raise suspicions as it is purely for defense.

Software is a place where some leaders can fall into a trap of thinking more is better. We have all heard people asking the question *what else do you need?* Piling more and more toolsets into a hunter's toolbox does not make them more effective. Instead, focus on the capabilities that exist first and become proficient at them before worrying about expanding.

Security information and event management

Unless the network that is being hunted on consists of only a single system, a **security information and event management (SIEM)** system is a must-have deployment requirement. This system can aggregate and correlate all of the logs ingested into it and make the identification of outlying behavior much easier.

When developing a SIEM template to use, it can be helpful to understand any existing rulesets utilized by the existing defenders on the network. If their SIEM is utilizing a different language than the teams, then the team can utilize tools such as **Uncoder** (`https://uncoder.io/`) that can translate queries and rulesets.

Some examples of common SIEM systems are as follows:

- Splunk

- Elastic

- Google Chronicle

- Azure Sentinel

- AlienVault OSSIM

While a SIEM can manage large scales of data in amazing ways, software can be employed to help retrieve some of those datasets in more unique ways that a dedicated piece of hardware might not be able to.

Passive network monitoring

It is possible for an adversary to hide so deep in a system that a team would not find them without significant targeted forensic analysis. However, it is not possible for an adversary to completely hide via the network, because they must send network traffic to communicate their actions.

This section covers the software that a team would install on a sensor connected to a SPAN or TAP in order to capture relevant network data. The software's main job would be to capture traffic, after that other software would be used to filter, alert, or remove unwanted data.

Some examples of common software-based network monitoring tools are as follows:

- Zeek (Bro)

- Suricata

What happens if just *monitoring* for adversarial behavior is not enough? If an organization needs to go to the next step and do a deeper level of monitoring closer to the source of the events? Many of these same types of systems can be used as **intrusion detection systems (IDSs)** or **intrusion prevention systems (IPSs)**.

Intrusion detection systems

An **IDS** goes beyond a standard antivirus in that it is normally signature- and heuristics-based. These different software solutions will normally exist on the same system the passive network monitoring tool is running on. An IDS differs from a passive network monitoring solution in that it can also generate alerts based upon what is identified. These can be collected at a later date or streamed back to a SIEM solution for ingestion.

Some examples of common IDS tools are as follows:

- Snort

- Suricata

If an organization wants to go one level further, many different IDSs that are deployed in-line (between the systems being monitored) can be converted to act as an **IPS**. This will allow them to automatically react when a certain event or threshold is met without having to worry about a defender giving the go-ahead. Instances like this can be much, much faster but at the same time dangerous if employed in the wrong manner. For this reason, an IDS is employed first before an IPS to baseline expected activity and minimize false positive triggering of the system.

Packet analysis

The analyst at some point will need to review the individual packets and longer communications that occur across the network. Depending upon the scope of the mission, a multitude of solutions exist, each with its own unique capabilities.

Some GUI-based examples are these:

- Arkime (Moloch)
- Wireshark

A command line-based example is this:

- TShark

While network analysis can come in many different flavors, there are very few *wrong* ways to do it. It always centers around how the hunter can analyze a large scale of data and identify the outlier that is an adversary. This is not the only source of helpful information; host systems producing that traffic can have a wealth of knowledge to be explored.

Host logging

Sometimes the host system is capable of producing logs, but just not at the right level of detail needed by the hunt team. Additional logging capabilities exist in tools that are designed to have a very low system impact while producing tailored logs for a defender. There must be a discussion with the network administrators about increased storage requirements for additional logs before pushing this software out to endpoints in the targeted network.

Some common third-party logging toolsets and data shippers are as follows:

- Sysmon (Windows)
- AgentD (Linux)
- RSYSLOG (Linux)
- Beats (or applicable SIEM agent for Windows and Linux)

When reviewing potential agents to employ, keep in mind that some also have a monetary cost to them as well. The decision to add agents to a system should be reviewed on a case-by-case basis. Each circumstance and environment is unique, based upon things such as what has already been observed on the network, what the normal toolsets employed by the administrators are, what will be utilized long term, and what the network is capable of supporting. If employed correctly, host-level logging will greatly enhance the capability of a hunt team to perform the next topic: host analysis.

Host analysis

At some point, the threat hunt team is going to have to examine data pulled from the workstations and servers on the organization's network. There are many different tools that the threat hunt team can choose from, some free and others requiring payment. This is not a host forensics book, and an analyst is going to need training to use any of this software due to the highly specialized nature of the tools for host forensics analysis, and the differences between endpoint operating systems.

Some common tools for threat hunt teams' host analysis are as follows:

- EZ tools (`https://ericzimmerman.github.io/`)
- Axiom
- Autopsy
- Sysinternals
- FTK
- SOF-ELK VM

Some teams choose to have dedicated systems that can employ all of these items. While this may make using them very simple and quick, it drives the cost of resources up. One solution to limiting what is required is to employ virtualization technologies such as Docker containers to quickly spin up or down select software.

Docker containers

While not mandatory for deployment, the use of software based Docker containers can make scaling out additional capabilities during a hunt, without requiring the addition of new hardware, an extremely easy and efficient task to accomplish. Additionally, if a standardized image is established for the team but not needed for all of the team, the individual members can quickly spin up a container for the item they need, utilize it, and then spin it back down once they are finished.

Many different images are freely available and maintained by a large community. If a need for the team arises, go to `https://hub.docker.com/` and see whether a solution already exists. Utilizing a public image is a very easy first step, but do not go into it blindly and default to trusting it to be perfectly secure. Always test the image in a closed environment to ensure it does not contain malicious or *noisy* configurations that the team does not want.

When choosing whether or not to use containers, remember that there are a dozen different scenarios that could be derived on how a virtualization technology such as this could be employed. Without getting too deep into all of the different technologies available, we will still review the high-level questions that will provide a direction on where the hunt team might need to go:

- Does the team want the system or program to be local to them, on a remote system they physically own, or in the cloud?
- Does the team want everything configured onto a single bare-bones system, a virtualized operating system, or independent virtualized applications?

A very common answer to these questions is that hunt teams want a local virtualized application, in which case, Docker fits the mold perfectly. If a cloud-based solution is needed instead, look for items referred to as a **Platform as a Service (PaaS)** offering. They can be very similar but have drastic differences when it comes to security, logging, and adherence to an organization's policies or various regulations.

Online versus offline system analysis

Another consideration to take into account when a team hunts on-site at an organization is that they might have the ability to conduct offline system analysis. Online system analysis is when a team analyzes a system while it is powered on and connected to the rest of the network. Offline analysis is when the system could be powered on, but not connected to the network anymore. Doing so will greatly lower the risk of the adversary discovering what was occurring.

One of the first rules in forensics should be followed in cases like this: never conduct analysis on your primary copy of data. For this scenario, when the system is offline make a copy of any items that the team would like to conduct analysis on. Hard drives can be simple enough as there are numerous cloners that will make exact duplicates. Imaging memory is a little trickier and requires interaction with the system in a powered-on state.

Regardless of what is duplicated, the team will need to work with the local administrators and decide whether the system that was analyzed should go back online. To not put it back exactly how it was could send a message to an adversary that is watching that something happened. If the system goes back online, but is reimaged with a fresh operating system, that will send a different message to an adversary. Be mindful of what is being communicated.

Regardless of whether online or offline system analysis is being conducted, there will be a very large set of data that is analyzed, and the results recorded. A case management solution will be where all of those results end up.

Case management

As previously covered, communication is critical, and keeping track of what analysts have found in addition to the other details of any investigations that are occurring will be key. There are plenty of case management solutions available, both free as well as paid.

Some examples for case management software or IR software packages are as follows:

- TheHive Project (`https://thehive-project.org/`)
- Security Onion (`https://securityonionsolutions.com/software`)
- SIFT Workstation (`https://www.sans.org/tools/sift-workstation/`)

While this has already been a lot of items to consider, more can be used to enhance the capabilities of the hunters throughout the mission. One such item is a threat intelligence platform that can be used to enrich existing data.

Threat intelligence ingestion platform

It will be up to the intelligence analyst to decide on what type of threat intelligence to ingest and how best to incorporate it for the team into the hunt. Just like with every other aspect of cybersecurity, ingestion can be automated and streamlined. One such example is a system called MISP, which is a standard solution that integrates with a lot of other paid and free SIEM products (`https://www.misp-project.org/`).

When integrating feeds, be careful about the type of feeds and configurations you have. Not all feeds are created equal, as they do not necessarily get *vetted* by anyone prior to publication. Additionally, ensure that the team does not *leak* customer data or alerts unless you have a specific reason and authorization to do so. For example, never upload files to VirusTotal unless both the team and the organization are alright with that file becoming available to anyone on the internet.

Sandboxes

A sandbox is an amazing addition to any cybersecurity defender's arsenal in fighting back against a threat actor. They will typically come in two different flavors: signature-based/static analysis and runtime analysis. A signature-based sandbox that conducts static analysis will look for known *strings* or *keywords* that are associated with malicious data. For example, if a file has the word `function Invoke-Mimikatz` as a string within the file, it could be the `Invoke-Mimikatz` PowerShell function. The actual method in which these sandboxes operate is significantly more complex; this scenario was given as a simplistic example.

A runtime sandbox will actually execute or open up the file that is being analyzed to record and report what happens. This is exceptionally helpful, as a lot of malware will be delivered in phases, with the first malware execution not actually containing anything malicious or any overt indications of its use. It is not until another computation is performed that the true intention is unencoded or downloaded.

When selecting the correct sandbox for your team or organization, there can be multiple solutions and they all have their own pros and cons. Some require additional equipment to stand up and manage. Some are free, while others have subscriptions. All these solutions have a cost, and it will not always be in the form of money; sometimes that cost is the resources to manage the system itself.

Some examples for sandbox systems are as follows:

- FireEye
- VirusTotal
- FileScan.IO
- Joe Sandbox
- Cuckoo
- Browser in the Box

In all, sandboxes are very valuable capabilities as they will ultimately answer a question that cannot be answered by reviewing logs alone. The sandbox will answer the question *What does this do?* Processing a script or file and seeing the results firsthand can save a lot of time and frustration in attempting to correlate logs for potential activity. *Seeing* a piece of malware execute and attempt to connect back to an adversarial server can quickly end all debates on what may have happened.

Scenario A – internal threat hunt

The team gets their war room ready using laptops and the servers that were previously decided upon. The team uses the network diagrams previously provided to determine the best location for sensors to gather interesting network data. First, they identify the enclaves they want to capture from, and then where the sensor would make the most sense, not just logically to ensure all traffic is captured, but physically as well. The sensors need to be placed in a location with adequate cooling and power, the same as any other IT device.

Once the sensor plan is determined, it is submitted to the stakeholders to determine whether there are any issues. Because of the legwork done by the legal team early in the hunt planning, there are no issues with the sensors being placed for the government-connected networks. However, the company is not willing to allow the hunt team to connect directly to the network and will be using out-of-band connections with TAPs that will be procured for the hunt team by the organization.

The software that is going to run on the sensors is Zeek, utilizing a baseline ruleset to capture traffic of interest to the hunt. This data will be pushed back to the war room hourly by some scripts the network administrator has set up. From there, the analysts will examine it on their laptops.

Logs from other endpoints, such as servers and workstations, will be requested from the security team and uploaded by the hunt team's administrator into the hunt network for analysis and correlation by analysts.

The hunt team has decided to have an *analyst network* and a *data network*. This will allow some separation between the operations and data storage, with some defense against accidental data tampering by an analyst. The router and switch necessary to do this were already on hand, and also set up by the administrator.

Tools that the analysts have decided on are based on their background and some quick training they were able to do online. Reviewing network traffic with Wireshark is tedious and time-consuming. The team wants to use it; however, with the timeframe they've been given, they'll need a tool to quickly compare traffic and try to find the malicious traffic to pinpoint Wireshark usage. For that, they're going to use an elastic stack with Arkime. This will run on the main server of the analyst network to speed the searches and drill-downs.

Also, on the server, they will use a Docker container of SNORT to process all the captured traffic through to quickly identify malicious network activities. The hunt team will use the baseline filters, which number in the thousands, in addition to building a few of their own based on the network architecture.

For host analysis, the team has decided to budget for some automated tools, since they're not experts and do need support and guidance during the host analysis portion. They decided to procure Axiom with a support contract to follow. The organization agreed to pay for this for 1 year to determine whether the ongoing hunt team is a worthwhile investment.

The team is unaware of case management solutions that can provide faster response and communication options during the hunt. They will be using their chat, whiteboard, and a shareable note-taking program (for example, OneNote) to track all the identified data and make assignments for tasks. These are the same tools the intelligence analyst will be using to attempt to share data with the whole team.

Scenario B – external threat hunt

CSI has the approval to connect directly to the IT network with their devices. As previously discussed, this will include utilizing technologies such as VPN, SSH, or HTTPS to connect to endpoints. The hunt team will further protect the network by utilizing a dedicated firewall appliance between the analyst network and the client network.

The client asked if CSI would be able to not just clear the IT network, which includes the OT control network, but the OT network itself. CSI threat hunters have no experience in OT and made it clear they would be just as big a threat on that network as a malicious actor. The team did provide alternate teams that are experienced in hunting on OT networks, which the stakeholders could engage in the future.

Because the teams are connecting directly, there's less bandwidth available for network data to flow continuously to the hunt team. This was discovered in planning and will require the hunt team to utilize more powerful sensors to do some of the filtering and analysis before sending data back for storage in the war room. These stronger sensors will have Zeek and Elastic installed on each, with SNORT and Suricata utilized in a container to do initial triage on the data that is being transmitted. Thankfully, the organization is allowing the use of TAPs instead of SPAN ports.

SPAN ports were originally selected by the client, but the overhead of sending all the traffic back through the network devices would have saturated them and the network links. This would have led to outages and poor network performance for the employees, which the stakeholders decided was untenable.

This team also utilizes an operational data network strategy for ensuring there's no corruption of the data that is saved for analysis by the team. The routers and switches used in the CSI networks are already procured by the team and included in part of the cost of the hunt.

The team will be utilizing a jump box that is in a new network segment, which was created just for the hunt in the client's network. This box will only have accounts for the hunt team members and have extra detection software installed (Sysmon) to forward all events to the hunt team to ensure there's no compromise.

The team will be using Splunk as the SIEM for network data ingestion to pinpoint where to further analyze network traffic. The analysts also have a fondness for the command-line tool TShark for packet analysis since it's faster and less processor-intensive on the laptops they'll be using.

Since the hunt team can connect directly to the impacted endpoints and do live analysis, they'll be using tools that are already in place there (for example, Event Viewer and Excel). However, if any data needs to be further examined for clues, they've been trained to use EZ tools for further analysis. Anything suspected to be a breach will be handed over to the security team as previously agreed.

The team will be using TheHive for case management, task assignment, and tracking of discovered indicators. TheHive also incorporates an intelligence-sharing platform, which the intelligence analyst will use to work with the team. However, there will be no utilization of the MISP or other data sharing capabilities because the client wants to ensure there's no accidental data leakage.

The team is not anticipating the need to detonate any malware found and, therefore, has determined not to set up and maintain a sandbox. If there is a need for that, they will utilize a separate contractor with client approval.

Summary

It's important to understand that the difference between an IT, OT, and cloud environment will be critical. If the team does not have experience in OT environments, then simply stay away from them. Do not be hesitant to ask questions as requirements are flushed out. This will help ensure that the team members with adequate experience and the proper equipment are deployed in support of the threat hunt.

Design the equipment needed for the hunt around the requirements and the network design. Do not decide on what is needed based upon what the team currently has available to them. There are a lot of different software solutions available to a team, both free and commercial. Default to living off of the land and utilizing what is already there. Build up from that existing baseline of capabilities and sources, then expand as needed to include new functionality and sources. While adding new sensors to get direct access to a log source might be the best solution, does an existing capability exist that could provide a secondary correlation of the same activity without changing the network configuration? Always be diligent and mindful of adding new items that change the baseline of the target network; as mentioned previously, everything you change can be observed by the adversary. They may respond to the new stimulus.

Now that equipment requirements and types have been outlined, we can move on to what the team will use that equipment for. This is what all of the planning and coordination has been for – data analysis, which we will discuss in the next chapter.

Review questions

Answer the following questions to check your knowledge of this chapter:

1. An example of a difference between an IT and OT network is that port scanning is normally fine on an _____ network whereas it could be detrimental on an ___ network.

2. Two of the biggest limiting factors of a cloud-based network are the ability to retrieve _____ and obtain _____.

3. If all communication from the hunt team is traversing the same network that the hunt is being conducted on, then that is an _____ connection.

4. If having to pick between a TAP or a SPAN, a _____ would be better put to use for an adversary that is believed to have infiltrated the existing infrastructure.

5. What are some common third-party host logging agents or data shippers?

Review answers

The answers to the review questions are as follows:

1. IT, OT

2. data or logs, authorization

3. in-band

4. TAP

5. Sysmon, AgentD, RSYSLOG, Beats

10
Data Analysis

Data is everywhere. When planning out a threat hunt there is a myriad of questions that will need to be answered. What types of data does the team need? Where does the team need to collect the data from? What data can the team live without and still be successful? There are three main methods of data collection to be followed. This chapter will cover all of those as well as different methods on how to perceive the data that is analyzed.

In this chapter, we are going to cover the following topics:

- Data collection mindsets
- Direct analysis versus secondary correlation
- Host logs versus network logs
- Automating everything
- Getting everyone on the same page
- Finding everything or nothing
- Scenario A - internal threat hunt
- Scenario B - external threat hunt

By the end of the chapter, you will be able to do the following:

- *Discuss* the different mindsets when it comes to data collection
- *Comprehend* the difference between direct analysis and secondary correlation
- *Comprehend* the importance of understanding the meaning of the data the team observes

Data collection mindsets

There are three typical mindsets when it comes to how a team plans on collecting data during a threat hunt as well as the general day-to-day defense of a network. They are as follows:

- **Input-driven**: Collect everything possible. If it has logs, then collect them and store them somewhere. The initial deployment of this method is low-effort as it just requires the added step of collecting existing logging. The downside of this mindset is that a defender can quickly be overloaded with information that does not matter.

- **Output-driven**: Collect and store only specific data that is known to the team and that they care about. This is a very tailored approach and requires the defender to know what to look for. While it is easy for an analyst to digest this method, they will immediately miss anything that is unknown to them without the ability to go back and retrieve it. This means if an incident responder or hunt analyst needs to review data that is not there, it may not exist any more as the data has been overwritten on the source system by the time this is realized.

- **Hybrid**: Collect whatever can be found and quickly begin to filter down from there. This method requires the highest level of effort among these three mindsets as it requires an upfront investment of time analyzing data to identify what is relevant and what is just background noise. The result is the best out of the three because the collection methodology will be a tailored experience by and for the team and that specific network.

Regardless of which method is employed, there is another concern to be mindful of – just because a team does not collect a data source immediately, does not mean that the data source should not or does not exist. Initial analysis can start in a **Security Information and Event Management (SIEM)** system where data is warehoused and processed. From there, data can almost always be retrieved from a host system after the initial analysis is performed. Therefore, the filtering of logs should begin early and often, starting with filtering on the host system that generated them.

An important aspect to keep in mind is that there is always a cost when moving data from one location to another. There are costs in resources such as bandwidth, time, storage, and processing power for encryption to secure the data from a host to the local collection point that the hunt team will use for data storage. Every time the same data is moved, there is another cost to move it; for example, from the hunt team storage location to a cloud instance where you might have other personnel that is assisting in the hunt. Ensure you weigh those costs against the benefit of moving the data and ensure that the expenditure is something that you are willing and able to pay.

Real-World Example

A team lead for a remote threat hunt was very interested in collecting all of the data available to them. They were able to work with the network owners to collect all of the available data that they could possibly obtain. For the team that was in the same physical location as the target network, this was not a problem as they had plenty of storage. However, the team lead also wanted to send all of this data back to a remote team for additional analysis.

The problem that they ran into was that the internet connection they had was just under 100 Mbps and was constantly down for half of the day. From a technical standpoint, it was just not possible to export the data in the manner and timeframe that the team needed. Instead, the team had to flex and identify what portions were necessary and only export those items.

In the end, the goal of the initial analysis performed on the SIEM system is to identify which activity is most likely a true positive and requires further investigation. From here, an analyst can return to the source systems to retrieve additional data and logs that were not originally sent to the SIEM device. The trade-off of this is that the source system may not have those logs anymore. A balance must be struck between capturing *all* logs and just the ones that are of initial interest to an analyst. It is an understood expectation of the follow-on investigation to require the retrieval of additional information.

Direct analysis versus secondary correlation

When a team analyzes data, there are two methods for the data to be analyzed and compared with other events. These two methods are direct analysis and secondary correlation:

- Direct analysis means going directly to the target source for information. If a system is believed to be running a malicious process, an analyst remoting into the system and viewing the running processes would be direct analysis.

- Secondary correlation means going back one step and inferring the state of a target without interacting directly with the target source. An analyst observing network traffic leaving a system and going to a known malicious command and control site would allow them to infer that the malicious code was being executed on the system.

Direct analysis will typically be observable by an adversary if they are looking for it. An analyst remoting into a system and running commands or even looking at the normal system-generated logs are all observable actions. Additionally, direct analysis by an analyst will usually leave evidence of the analyst's actions behind on the endpoint. This could expose credentials, imply intent, and will change the data on the system. Understand that whether performing direct analysis with the built-in toolsets and logs or utilizing a toolset that does its own analysis on the system will have the same results in that it will be observable by anyone already monitoring and would most likely change the state of the system. This direct analysis allows confirmation of whether an activity does or does not exist by removing the assumption that an action took place as it was either observed or was not. This is the cost of direct analysis; the system is modified by looking at it.

Secondary correlation cannot be observed from the target source as the analyst is never on the target. However, by doing so, the analyst cannot always be positive that a specific event did or did not occur as it will require *logical assumptions*. For example, if an analyst observes an abnormal network traffic pattern sent from a system to a known malicious site at a steady tempo, they can assume that it is malicious software, but it is not possible to prove that without direct analysis or additional corroboration.

> **Real-World Example**
>
> During a threat hunt, traffic was observed from a known SSH botnet attempting to connect to a particular system. Reviewing the network traffic, attempted logins were observed at a regular tempo. The question was asked by leadership, *Did the adversary get into the system?* Based upon secondary correlation, the assessment back to leadership was that no traffic was observed leaving the targeted system that fit the standard handshake for a successful SSH connection and it was not believed that any unauthorized access into the system had occurred.
>
> After the intrusion was fully stopped and the system was isolated, the target system was reviewed. The system logs identified repeated password failures from that botnet and confirmed through direct analysis that the adversary was not able to gain a foothold.

Both direct analysis and secondary correlation have their places within a hunt. It is not always prudent or possible to directly observe activity on the endpoint. Assumptions and inferences will have to be made. This is where proper planning will pay off by providing the team with the data and assurances to accurately make these assessments even if they cannot be seen directly.

With a proper data analysis plan in place, the team will need to discuss and decide what *type* of data to retrieve. Should they concentrate on host-level data, network-level data, or a balance of the two. The next section will dive into some thoughts on how to attack this evolving issue.

Host logs versus network logs

When it comes to log sources, they are normally broken up into two categories: host-based and network-based logs. Host logs would contain anything found on a host or application such as the operating system. Included in this category would be anything generated by toolsets employed by cyber defense such as any **Endpoint Detection and Response (EDR)** toolsets they are utilizing. Network logs would be anything that is captured as it is traveling across the network, such as the raw packets communicated on an enterprise.

Does a team need them both? Can a team hunt off of primarily one of them? The answer to how to address this balance is it all depends upon the hunt team and what is already available to them. Is it possible to conduct a threat hunt with only host logs and data? Yes. Is it also possible to conduct a threat hunt with only network logs and data? Yes. If a team has specialized or a deeper understanding of a particular area, exploit that to their advantage. If there has to be a choice between something the team can immediately use and find valuable versus something that may prove valuable down the road, pick the one that has the best return on investment.

Part of that balance should also include what is naturally available based on the existing architecture of the network. If collecting network traffic and logs is a trivial thing while collecting host-based logs will take a larger effort by the team, weigh up whether that investment of resources is necessary. If it is, decide exactly how much is needed. While the team may want host-level logs, antivirus logs, and archived logs in a backup, they may have to settle for only having the antivirus logs initially and rely more on the network data available to them. If a system or systems are found to be of interest, do not hesitate to reassess and change course. For those few systems, it could be worthwhile investing time and energy into retrieving that additional data.

Now that the team has reviewed where logs can originate from and how they can be prioritized, the team will move on to the next phase of any IT job – automation. This is where a team is able to dive deep and quickly digest large amounts of information in short time periods. If there is anything the team does more than once, always consider automating that task.

Automating everything

There is a rule of thumb for anything in information technology, which is – if you have to do it more than once, then that task should be automated. When it comes to data analysis, the direction is no different. Whenever possible, push all of your relevant data into a SIEM for large-scale aggregation, correlation, and analysis. Manual analysis and correlation are extremely difficult and time-consuming. As the amount of data increases, this task becomes closer to impossible for a group of analysts to do efficiently without some form of automation.

By utilizing technologies such as a centralized SIEM, even if it is central only to the hunt team, tasks stop being repeated. After initial SIEM deployment, a hunt operator can build a custom query for identifying DNS command and control for a customer's network, lateral movement, or suspicious host logins if that data is ingested. From there, the data should be put into the SIEM that automatically runs the query on a scheduled timeline and alerts the hunt operators if it is ever triggered. A single individual manually running the same query repeatedly and analyzing the results would be an extreme waste of resources.

Invest the team's time into customizing dashboards or notebooks in order to allow them to automate common queries. These will normally be automated queries that will be able to turn into visualizations within the SIEM, which further aids in identifying outlying anomalies through graphical representation that is easier for an analyst to review, great for final reports, and in the end, a fantastic product that can be handed over to the long-term defenders of the network to continue the search for adversarial activity.

As the threat hunt progresses, more and more general analyses and reviews will become automated. As the timeline expands, it will be very easy for operators to lose focus of what is happening in the background. In this next section, we will discuss how to ensure all of the stakeholders continue to remain on the same page in understanding what is occurring and what is required to happen next.

Getting everyone on the same page

The ability of a team lead to keep the whole team in sync with one another is a monumental task. Accomplishing this becomes much easier when you take into account the benefits of proper data collection, day-to-day communication, and documentation. Take the time and ensure that the team conducts pre-briefs and debriefs for each shift. Before starting the shift, every team member should be up to speed on what happened previously and what everyone needs to do on the oncoming shift. Before leaving for the day, everyone should review what was accomplished and agree on the planned activities for the following shift. A team member should never get to the point of saying *I'm not sure what to do next*.

Additionally, analysts will need the ability to pivot off of each other's data and findings on a regular basis. This starts with ensuring that the proper team environment is established so that everyone can easily and naturally access data that is ingested into the team. Scrolling through 5 days' worth of chat to find a log file that was posted is more resource-intensive for an analyst than having all data ingested into a single SIEM where it is ready to be correlated.

Little things that a team lead can do to make the management of data and communication better can pay major dividends throughout the execution of the hunt. Never hesitate to perform an action or activity that improves communication within the team and helps members understand the data that they are reviewing.

From here, we will move on to the final concept that needs to be understood when it comes to data analysis. It is very likely that a team might find no evidence of malicious activity on a network even though they did all of the *things* that they had planned to do. Let's dive into what this means to the team and the hunt as a whole.

Finding everything or nothing

Whether or not an analyst ends up finding the golden nugget that is an adversary at all is not proof of a successful threat hunt. This is due to the fact that a lack of evidence of identifiable adversary activity is not proof of no adversary being present. The focus should be kept on the hypothesis while noting items of interest for the customer to follow up with. Completion of objectives and tasks along with efficiency and their completeness are the best measurements of the team's success.

Scenario A – internal threat hunt

The team works through their plan and uses their **Cyber Management Framework (CMF)** to start collecting data from the network for analysis. Due to the resources provided by Widget Makers Inc., they have decided to collect all the data they can off of any device that the team has access to and comb through it later. If there is a system on the target network that produces logs, they will attempt to obtain those logs for later analysis.

Thankfully, the administrator for the team's equipment really understood what this meant for the data to be hand-processed by a team of relative security novices. They built a SIEM on one of the spare servers. The data from the sensors will import directly into this SIEM after passing through the other detections first. This streamlines the data processing and allows the hunters to get to work faster.

Due to the configuration of the hunters' out-of-band analysis network, the team will gain additional efficiency in long-term analysis by utilizing the SEIM. This stops the data from having to be moved continuously from the data network to the analyst network since the SEIM will allow the analysts to review the data and pinpoint what they actually need to examine deeper from the data network.

As the team starts analyzing the evidence, they start to see strange network activity coming from workstations that shouldn't be connecting directly to the internet. After some questions were posed to the **Network Operations Center** (**NOC**) and **Security Operations Center** (**SOC**), the team learns these endpoints weren't supposed to have direct connections to the internet, but no one ever set up blocks to prevent them from happening. Additionally, these endpoints are running an operating system that is almost old enough to vote.

However, they're not allowed to examine these devices for some time due to compliance controls in place to protect the organization. So, they're only able to observe the secondary correlation and log the need to get additional information from the workstation itself. This is also logged with the SOC as a possible priority investigation.

There is evidence of these endpoints connecting to normal workstations though. The team can get the logs of those workstations and examine the endpoints directly. These workstations are a current operating system with excellent security controls and auditing. However, the auditing policy set for Widget Makers Inc. is not capturing all the necessary activities to assist in the hunt. The direct examination for evidence continues, but the team notifies the NOC of the need for an emergency change to alter the auditing policy for all devices on the network.

As the team finds indicators of interest and shares those with the NOC and SOC, they also update a *correlation table* in their group note-taking software. The administrator then uses this to build additional alerts into the SIEM. This automation stops each analyst from having to constantly search for the same **Indicators of Compromise** (**IOCs**) during each portion of the investigation. Additional automation takes place on the sensors to tag data for easier sorting in the data storage network. This was done by hand as it manually transferred to the team by the administrator but took an excessive amount of time since the team wanted to collect all the data possible.

The team starts meeting three times a day briefly to go over the past few hours of activity, set objectives for the next work period, and ensure there's no missed communication. OneNote is working fine, but the team lead is not happy with how work assignments are being tracked and communicated. They've tasked the team to look for a case management solution to streamline their tasking, IOC collection, and sharing capabilities.

The team has started to find things based around their hypothesis, but no smoking guns and nothing to hand off yet to the SOC for a deep investigation. The team lead reminds them that expectations were set that they might not find anything pointing directly to what's causing the issues, but they'd already identified changes that greatly increase the security of Widget Makers Inc.

Scenario B – external threat hunt

Due to the **Cyber Security Intelligence** (**CSI**) team setting up stronger sensors at the beginning and the lack of bandwidth for data collection, the team must use a hybrid approach to get the evidence. The sensors will be able to filter ahead of time for items they don't need, and the small selection of data they want full copies of can be sent directly via the jump box.

They have automatic tagging set up and dashboards built out of the box for the most common ways the team is going to analyze the data for evidence to prove their hypothesis. Other items that are automated are taking IOCs from TheHive and scripting them to be built into simple detections for the SIEM.

As the team starts searching across the network for evidence to test their hypothesis, they identify a workstation that's reaching out to other workstations across the network with no reason to do so.

They're able to see the secondary correlation evidence in the network traffic and are able to examine the workstation directly using the jump box. The evidence is compiled and added to TheHive and identified to the security team. The team lead has made strong efforts to ensure working with the security team is very smooth, including inviting them to the end-of-day meetings.

The team continues to build new dashboards in the SIEM to tailor them to the organization's unique schema and the evidence they find along the way. This iterative update speeds the hunt along as non-relevant data is excluded from the analysis until it's determined that it is relevant the further the hunt progresses.

The team lead has regular updates with the clients where the language is very clear and based on the evidence. Expectations for the hunt are constantly reinforced to state the team can only hunt on the evidence available, and there may not be any findings related to the issues going on. The CSI hunt team understands these outcomes based on experience.

Summary

Remember, there are three types of data collection. Input-driven data collection is about collecting everything possible, output-driven data collection involves collecting only what is known and important, and finally, hybrid data collection starts with collecting all the data and then quickly narrowing it down. Direct analysis is seeing something at the source that proves or disproves an occurrence. Secondary correlation is observing evidence outside of the target system and inferring what occurred.

When it comes to conducting this type of work, always automate correlation and analysis as much as possible in order to free up the team's primary resource: time. In the end, finding or not finding the adversary is not necessarily a sign of success. Stick to what the purpose of the threat hunt is, and the objectives laid out during planning.

In the next chapter, we will dive into what is produced by all of this data analysis – documentation. It is a good thing to review data and understand what happens but those findings will quickly be lost without proper documentation by the team.

Review questions

Answer the following to check your knowledge of this chapter:

1. _____-driven collection methods are concerned with collecting and storing only the things that are known to the team and that they might care about.
2. _____-driven collection methods are concerned with collecting and storing everything possible.
3. _____ collection methods are concerned with a combination of the other two.
4. (True or False) Secondary correlation is making an inference about something without directly observing it.
5. (True or False) When conducting a threat hunt, the main goal that matters is finding an adversary.

Review answers

The answers to the review questions are as follows:

1. Output-driven

2. Input-driven

3. Hybrid

4. True

5. False: the focus should always be on proving or disproving the hypothesis of the hunt

11
Documentation

If it has not been clear thus far in this book, communication is an exceedingly important concept to understand at this point. Communication is key at each step of a threat hunt. If any member of the team and organization fails to effectively communicate, then they can cause the entire team and organization to incur a penalty, leading to a potential threat-hunt failure.

Communication in the short term can be accomplished in many different forms. However, long-term communication—for example, an understanding that will last more than an hour—needs to be recorded for future reference. Take to heart the following rule: *If it isn't written down, then there is no evidence that it did or did not occur.* This applies to everyone: threat-hunt team members, individuals in leadership roles, and organizational stakeholders.

While there are a large number of potential documentation areas that a team would want to document, things such as a daily and monthly hunting schedule and standard detection rules are a great thing for a team to have. Without going into the weeds on some of the standard team-based documentation, we will focus on higher-level requirements that could be unique to a hunt team.

In this chapter, we are going to cover the following topics:

- Processes and procedures
- **Memorandum of agreement (MOA)**
- **Statement of work (SOW)**
- Authorities
- Pre-approved actions
- Scenario A—internal threat hunt
- Scenario B—external threat hunt

By the end of the chapter, you will be able to do the following:

- *Identify* the high-level processes and procedures used during a threat hunt
- *Comprehend* the importance of having an MOA
- *Discuss* the appropriate authorities needed during a hunt
- *Comprehend* how pre-approved actions are integrated into the team's actions

Processes and procedures

When it comes to documentation, the most basic communication to document will be operator **tactics, techniques, and procedures (TTPs)**. These are the day-to-day and minute-to-minute actions that operators and analysts take throughout the life cycle of a threat hunt. To break this down further, think of TTPs like this:

- **Tactic**: A general concept or way of approaching a problem.

  Example: Performing a **denial-of-service (DoS)** attack against a target.

- **Technique**: Narrower in focus than a tactic, should include specific mechanisms used to accomplish the required action.

  Example: Performing a DoS attack using **Low Orbit Ion Cannon (LOIC)** on port 80/**Transmission Control Protocol (TCP)**.

- **Procedure**: Very specific directions, requirements, and toolsets an individual would follow to achieve the desired outcome. These are typically tested, honed, and verified prior to use on client networks.

  Example: Step-by-step directions on how to configure and utilize LOIC for a DoS attack.

Real-World Example

An organization recently underwent a high turnover of hunt operators, leaving most positions occupied by newer analysts. While all members were highly technical and experienced in defensive cybersecurity, they were brand new to working as a team and had no documentation on how the organization conducted hunt operations. Each was presented with the following question: *How would you identify if an adversary had logged on to a remote system?*

When the four members were asked this question, four different answers were returned, and each member suggested using different toolsets that in turn provided a different level of assurance on the actual activity taking place. Members were asked a follow-up question about the other toolsets their teammates would use. Viewpoints on the effectiveness of each other's methods were again all over the place. This was one of the leading causes of the difficulties they experienced during hunts, replicating their findings day after day.

Something as simple as a lack of a documented process for analyzing data led to a massive separation in how the team members operated. Once TTPs were established, the team began to operate in a repeatable manner that could be matured further.

In our experience, there are typically three main ways of considering processes' and procedures' documentation, as outlined next. The hunt team will need to have previously established where they view their operational maturity to be and hold each other accountable to the standard that they have established:

- **Documentation is required for everything**: "All TTPs must be fully documented and approved by leadership prior to use on a customer's network. There are very few exceptions, and those exceptions have an emergency approval process outlined for temporary use."

The idea of documenting *all* TTPs in detail may seem a daunting task, and it is. However, while the level of detail included will be different from team to team, the end goal will be the same: do not execute a tactic on a target network whose concept has not been tested. This will allow the underlying goal—reducing risk as much as possible—to be achieved.

This type of documentation standard can be very beneficial for any hunt or environment with extremely low risk tolerance. If the client organization or hunt team cannot risk any potential impact to the enterprise, then this is the documentation standard to utilize. The key here requiring full documentation is that the risks of testing out new tactics or methodologies cannot be accepted within the enterprise or with customers' data that is not backed up. However, if multiple copies of the customers' data exist and backup restoration has proven successful, then the risk level is modified to low, and experimental TTPs could be performed against a copy of that particular dataset.

The positive side is that almost all work is done ahead of the hunt. During execution, it would just be a matter of applying all the planning and TTPs to the dataset with no deviation. This plan should always include methods for reducing false positives that are initially identified, along with how to obtain any additional data that might be needed once a system of interest is identified. The negative side of this approach is that the operators have very little—if any—flexibility during the hunt. If a new opportunity that was not foreseen during planning presents itself, then the hunters will not be able to deviate to exploit it. The intended audience for this level of documentation is generally inexperienced operators as only prescribed actions are approved; however, the level of risk acceptable will dictate applicability.

- **Documentation is a crutch**: "Each individual has their own method of performing actions. By not prescribing what an operator can or cannot do, they are able to more freely maneuver across the cyber landscape to achieve their goal."

This is in the extreme opposite documentation direction. High-level documentation should still exist from the planning session on the various tactics that will be employed on client networks; an example would be examining registry data from a Windows endpoint. However, past that level of guidance, little will exist for techniques, and there will definitely be no documentation for procedures. Instead, resources will be dedicated to enabling operators to hone their own procedures that fit their hunt style.

This can be beneficial in a hunt and enterprise that has a medium-to-high level of risk tolerance. A great example of a common practice with this documentation approach would be a threat-hunting exercise. While employing this method is definitely easier, it is highly unadvisable during a live hunt as it goes against the principles of good communication. Each operator can, and probably will, utilize different techniques and procedures. No standard approach will be utilized across the team, and the outcome could be different based on the analyst who performed the action. The intended audience for this documentation concept would be extremely experienced operators.

The long-term impact is that team members will grow into stove-piped areas of expertise, and the team will eventually have those one or two individuals who do most things, with no one else understanding how it is done. The team will not grow and mature. Again, it is highly recommended against using this method anywhere outside of a training environment.

- **Set boundaries**: "Approved tactics and techniques should be documented. The detailed procedures on how to accomplish them can be left up to the operator."

This method establishes a left and right boundary for the threat-hunt team on what they can and cannot execute. Any activity within those boundaries is approved for execution, and they can approach this as they see fit. This approach allows for planning and detailed communication with a client on general actions to be performed while leaving open the ability to discuss business risks. If there is a particular tactic that presents too much risk to the enterprise, then the teams' *boundaries* can be modified to modify or exclude it completely.

The establishment and holding of boundaries is the recommended method for the vast majority of threat hunts. The intended audience for this documentation concept is a good mix of experienced and inexperienced operators.

If the documentation portion of this is new to the team, then start with the foundations and align everyone to using the same terms, methodology, and performant expectations. From there, move on and start producing best practices that people can use as options based on the situation. If three different tools could be used for a specific technique, then the team should discuss and document the pros and cons of each so that it is clear to all members when they should or should not use them.

An example of this would be documenting that tool *A* used in a particular way is extremely accurate and hardest to hide from; however, it is easily visible if an adversary is still present in the network. Tool *B* can also work but at a slower pace, and it is possible for an advanced adversary to fake the results it provides. However, tool *B* does not interact directly with the system, and it would be extremely hard for an adversary to identify it was being employed. The following screenshot shows a sample way of documenting a team's TTPs:

CSI Threat Hunt TTP

Threat Hunt TTP Reference – 2.0.1

Incident Response Reference – 3.1

Tactic – Clear endpoint of threat actor activity (windows)

Purpose – Determine if there has been threat actor activity on a suspected endpoint due to hypothesis or evidence of suspicious behavior.

Technique – Utilization of forensics tools and log reviewing clear the endpoint of threat actor activity

Purpose – The endpoint will require analysis of forensics and log data using tools specific to the endpoint. Windows tools available to use, but not required, are:

Online Sources -

    EZ Tools - https://ericzimmerman.github.io/#!index.md

    Excel – Office Suit

    EventLogExplorer - https://eventlogxp.com/

    FTK - https://www.exterro.com/forensic-toolkit

    Volatility - https://github.com/volatilityfoundation/volatility

All tools are available at the tool share on the forensics network at "Z:\Forensics\Tools" for local download.

Tactic – Review logs for threat actor access and activities.

    Log review – Use EventLogExplorer by.....(command, configuration, suspect output)

Tactic – Analyze memory for indicators of compromise, exfiltration, network connections

    Memory review – Utilize volatility on a Linux VM to...(command, configuration, suspect output)

Tactic – Use EZ Tools to review forensics data from endpoint for indicators of threat actor activity

    EZ tool MFTExplorer – Configuration; "command to use"; suspect output;

Figure 11.1 – Sample TTP documentation

With a daily documentation methodology in place, there are other types of standard documents that the team will need to be aware of. In the next section, we will cover the concept of an MOA, which lays out the foundation of the team's place within the target organization.

MOA

Whatever written agreements might be called within an organization, there should always be a formalized and signed agreement between the hunt team and the organization's stakeholders who own and operate the target enterprise. In the case of a threat hunt, this typically starts with a formal request for assistance that allows for discussions to begin. This formal request can be as simple as an email to a sales mailbox, or a formal written **request for proposal** (**RFP**). Then, negotiations start to determine the resources that will be made available to the threat-hunt team. If those negotiations go well and a threat hunt is determined to be value-added and beneficial to the organization, then planning will begin.

Upon conclusion of planning, a deliverable is due to all parties in the form of a signed/approved plan that specifies all the requirements and expectations of the threat hunt. This is where the items that were painstakingly laid out, drilled, and refined in *Chapter 7, Planning*, are presented to the client. As much as possible, each expected phase of the hunt should be made clear to all parties and will include what can, cannot, will, and will not be accomplished by all parties. Additionally, it should also be conveyed how the deliverables for each phase of the hunt will be identified, communicated, and assigned to individuals able to perform the required actions.

Once again, it is all about communication, with the new requirement of clear documentation! Have those difficult and uncomfortable discussions upfront during the planning session, have everyone agree to them, and then *write it all down*. These communication challenges are much easier to deal with when there is not an adversary than dealing with communication problems while the team is also interacting with an adversary. The following screenshot shows a sample MOA that displays a common format. This is just a sample—the one employed by your threat-hunting team could take any form that meets your own requirements:

Widget Maker, Inc

Memorandum of Agreement

Subject: Threat Hunting Engagement

1) Widget Maker, Inc executive leadership and board of directors have determined an organic threat hunt is in the best interest of the organization and has designated Mr. Name as the lead for this effort.

2) Mr. Name will select a team to stand up this effort from the Network Operations Center and the Security Operations Center. His first tasks are:

    a. Develop a timeline for the threat hunt engagement
    b. Develop a communication plan to adhere to during this effort.

3) The initial budget for this effort is: $#,###. Space will be allocated in building 104, Rm 3. Initial equipment will be supplied from IT, with the budget directed towards additional items and tools as Mr. Name determines necessary.

4) The hunt will take place from dd/mm/yyyy to dd/mm/yyy. The phases of the hunt will be determined by Mr. Name as part of the timeline development.

5) All actions, analysis, hypotheses, and requests will be approved by the CIO Mrs. Name as long as they do not impact NETWORK. For those actions impacting NETWORK Mrs. Name and our legal partner Ms. Name will work together to find solutions and present them to the executive team for adjudication.

CEO	Threat Hunt Lead
Date _____	Date _____
Signature _____	Signature _____
Name/Title _____	Name/Title _____

1347 NORTHSIDE LANE, GOTHAM, IL 96704
HTTP://WWW.WIDGETMKR.COM

Figure 11.2 – Sample MOA

What if the team that is coming to do the threat hunt isn't an internal team and is external to the organization, or what if the team is from a separate division within a large organization and funding lines are involved? That's where an *SOW* can come to be utilized instead of an MOA. This next section will cover this concept in detail, along with providing a sample of what one could look like.

SOW

An MOA can be used for arrangements with parties outside the organization, but that is not common business practice. SOWs are used between businesses to record what kind of work will be done and which deliverables are expected.

The communication here isn't limited to the work the team will do, but also must at a minimum discuss compensation, possibly some of the tactics, and other communication requirements. The construct and specificity of the SOW will depend on what each party wants the document to say. For example, it could just state that a forensics/threat-hunting company will perform *forensics services* for up to a certain amount of money. An SOW will almost always have a set amount of money for the threat-hunting firm to spend— this is because it's a commercial agreement. Open-ended engagements are not common within the cybersecurity industry because teams can always keep hunting due to the never-ending supply of data, but no organization has the funds to support an endless 24/7 hunt—if they did, it would be cheaper to make the team in-house.

Common items to list in an SOW are provided here:

- **Compensation**: The amount of money to be paid to the external threat-hunting team for their engagement with the requesting organization.

- **Time frame of the engagement**: Start and end dates, or an estimation, to ensure there is some force behind the agreement. This ensures the stakeholder and threat-hunt team will not delay the engagement.

- **Date when the allocated funds will expire**: A date when the funds are considered spent, and the outside organization will no longer receive services. Often during an engagement, there are individuals who do not support the hunt. This provision is to ensure the team does get compensated for their efforts, even if a hunt never happens due to the requesting organization's negligence.

- **Operating processes**: Sometimes, an SOW is requested to detail how data is transferred, analyzed, or stored. Often, this is to comply with organizational certifications (for example, the **Cybersecurity Model Maturity Certification (CMMC)**, **Systems and Organization Controls version 2 (SOCv2)**, and so on). Processes can be listed in the SOW to ensure they're enforced and meet compliance requirements.

- **Deliverables**: What is the external team going to provide at the end of the hunt? It is important to list deliverables at the beginning so that time can be budgeted for this and all stakeholders know what is going to be produced. Please note that deliverables can change through the course of a hunt. If threats are found and lawyers are engaged, they could dictate that a comprehensive report is no longer desired due to the legal implications once the hunt is done.

- **Communication methods**: List out the common communication means that the external team will use during the hunt. As discussed in *Chapter 4, Communication Breakdown*, keeping all parties in sync is extremely important. Listing communication methods in the SOW can set expectations.

Similar to the previous screenshot, the following screenshot is merely a sample. The SOW should be customized to whatever is applicable to the team's organization and expected purposes:

STATEMENT OF WORK FOR THREAT HUNT WITH CUSTOMER

MONTH #, YEAR

SERVICES	TYPE
THREAT HUNTING • Work will be accomplished remotely|on-site with provided space • Development of hypotheses related to network and host indicators based on indications • Collection of network traffic and endpoint data (from span ports or taps) at key points, for approved portions of the network • Ongoing intelligence collection against COMPANY information • Analysis and correlation of all indicators of security impacts • Development of communications plan for the threat hunt **Deliverables** • Deliver a Cyber Intelligence Brief on details found during the threat hunt • Delivery of timed reports as COMPANY requires • Final report delivered 30 business days after completion of hunt **Dates** • Projected start and end date – dd/mm/yyyy - dd/mm/yyyy • Projected report delivery date – dd/mm/yyyy • **Projected funds expiration – dd/mm/yyyy**	$XX,XXX

The Services described above are being purchased by COMANY for its benefit from CSI Int'l (CSI). Hereafter referred to as "Parties" together.

It is the understanding of the Parties that the COMPANY is a signatory of the Statement of Work (SOW). CSI agrees to make reasonable business efforts to ensure that COMPANY complies with all duties, responsibilities, obligations, etc., assigned to it within this SOW.

Through this SOW the COMPANY authorizes CSI to start a Threat Hunting and Investigation engagement which will consist of, but not be constrained to, threat hunting, cybersecurity threat investigations, intelligence services, recommendation, and report generation at a COMPANY desired confidentiality level.

The SOW begins once CSI receives a signed SOW and Purchase Order from the COMPANY.

CSI will invoice COMPANY according to the terms of COMPANY's signed SOW for this program. Payment is due from COMPANY within 30 days of the receipt of the invoice.

CSI	COMPANY
Date _____	Date _____
Signature _____	Signature _____
Name/Title _____	Name/Title _____

CSI, Intl.
www.csi-intl.com

Figure 11.3 – Sample SOW

With the SOW drafted, the final lines on the document will be a significant consideration. The individuals that sign this item must be the same ones that can provide authorization for those activities. Failure to do so could land the team in some precarious legal situations. In the next section, we will cover in more detail what this means and who those individuals are.

Authorities

The requirement for clear authorities to work in a client's network can make or break any hunt team. Determining authorities is the responsibility of the team lead to ensure the threat hunt is legitimate and approved on an infrastructure identified for activities.

Just because someone says that you can do something does not mean that you can do that thing.

Sometimes, this rather simple concept can be one of the most difficult parts of a threat hunt. It can be extremely difficult to figure out who has the authority to grant permission to perform threat-hunt actions. The requirement for formal and written permission is to agree that hunt team members won't be going to jail for approved activities. While this might sound like a far-fetched scenario, it is not.

> **Real-World Example**
>
> In 2019, an Iowa-based cybersecurity organization was contracted by the state to conduct penetration tests of some of their municipal facilities, including a courthouse. During one of the tests, two of the members were arrested and jailed. The issue, the county stated, was that the building was in their jurisdiction and not state-level government's. Due to this, the state's approval to conduct the penetration test was not legal and the members were performing unauthorized—and therefore criminal—activities against the county facilities (https://www.cnbc.com/2019/11/12/iowa-paid-coalfire-to-pen-test-courthouse-then-arrested-employees.html).

If the hunt team is an outside firm, then lawyers should always be involved at some point to verify the proper authorities and paperwork are in order. Skipping this step is the equivalent of playing roulette with fines, spending time in jail, and acquiring a bad public reputation. Once the authorities are clear that permissions for the threat hunt have been established by the appropriate stakeholder, the lead is responsible for ensuring the team does not exceed the identified boundaries. If the client requests actions that were not previously approved or lays out a clear pathway for approval, then the answer from the threat-hunt team is simply *no*. New authorizations should be given in writing to expand any permitted activities before any are taken beyond the original scope of allowance. Keep in mind that the specifics of what the pathway to approval is and how authority expansion takes place will be different for each and every hunt.

The inverse of this is much easier to accomplish. If either the customer or the hunt team wants to refrain from something that was previously approved, then that is allowed to happen. During the negotiation process, this eventuality will need to be described, along with the spin-down time required to restrict those actions and authorities, as large amounts of data and deployed sensors cannot cease to exist at the snap of a finger. Identify and agree ahead of time who can expand authorities, who can restrict authorities, any causes for the emergency ceasing of operation, and the expected timetable for those subsequent actions to take place.

Here is a sample list of things to include in an authorization:

- Authorizing agent
- Recipient of authorization (hunt team)
- Time period authorization is valid for (explicit dates and/or time frames)
- Location authorized for the hunt (physical, logical, and so on)
- Data the team is authorized to interact with
- Any explicit unauthorized actions/activities/data/locations
- Any authorized (pre-approved) actions that require notification to the customer
- Identification of which authorized actions require prior notification and which can be notified after they occur
- Methods and time frames for modification of authorization
- Dated signatures of all parties

While these types of authorities outline the *general* concepts that the hunt team will follow, there can be more detailed considerations that the team will run into. These concepts fall into a category referred to as *pre-approved actions*. In this next section, we will cover the different types of actions and how they are integrated into the overall plan.

Pre-approved actions

All actions that the hunt team will take will fall into one of three categories, as follows:

- **Normal activities**: These are low-threat, routine, typical daily actions—an example of this is an operator reviewing data collected overnight that was automatically ingested into the **security information and event management (SIEM)** device. These types of activities typically carry with them a low risk to the data, the enterprise, and the threat-hunt operation. No additional approval is needed from the customer or the lead before an operator performs them.

- **Pre-approved actions**: These are actions that increase overall risk (exposure, detection, the risk to the network, and so on) and require notification to the team's leadership that they were or are about to be executed. Depending upon the agreement with the client, these actions might also require notification to the organizational stakeholders that they were executed. An example could be interacting with a machine that is exhibiting signs of remote **command and control (C2)**. While this should be expected from a client standpoint, the team lead will definitely be interested in these actions and want to ensure full coordination.

- **Non-approved actions**: These are actions that drastically increase overall risk (exposure, network, and so on) and require permission from the customer before executing them. A great example of this would be closing a firewall port that an adversary is conducting C2 through that could block operationally necessary traffic.

Ensure examples of each category are well documented and understood by all parties taking part in the threat hunt. As the hunt team matures, they will be able to slowly build up lists of what these items are. Documentation of these lists will allow the team to train to expand established standards and communicate more effectively with one another as well as the client.

Scenario A – internal threat hunt

Widget Maker's team started compiling activities they wished to conduct during the hunt early on in the planning phase. These were gleaned from online sources (for example, `https://www.sans.org/white-papers`) and in the individual training and studying team members had done on their own. The team lead developed a template to start recording all these activities so that they could be standardized. However, there wasn't enough time between when this collection and documentation started, and the hunt needed to start.

The MOA that was shared between the stakeholders and the team included general tactics the hunt team would take, and from that selection, a few were explicitly approved, forming the basis for pre-approved actions the team could take. All other activities had to be presented to the team lead and get approved before being allowed to be conducted on the network. That approval process was not documented in the MOA, and during the start of the hunt, this was identified as a significant gap. The team lead spent a day with stakeholders, trying to identify where all the authorities lay to determine who to get approval from. Those authorities were agreed to in an appendix to the MOA that everyone also dated and signed.

For most activities, the team would need permission from the security team and the network team. If either one of those entities was not comfortable about approving the activities, it would then go to the **chief executive officer** (**CEO**) for approval. This was for all network enclaves except for the government one, which included additional permissions from lawyers at each step. Once this agreement was done, there were sometimes still long delays in waiting for approval, but the team moved along in the hunt and cataloged the activities they were waiting for and included this information in all meetings with stakeholders to attempt to pressure quicker resolutions.

As the hunt progressed, the team leader identified that different information was being provided for what should have been the same techniques and procedures. Due to the immaturity of the team, many members were using their own tools and scripts to get the information needed for the hunt. However, the results didn't always conform to the documentation standards. The team lead worked with members to identify which tools provided information that was required for the deliverables that were due at the end of the hunt. Members slowly started moving over to the same tools and procedures.

Scenario B – external threat hunt

As the team moves throughout the hunt, they're using the processes and procedures they've used for other clients and hunts without issue. CSI is a mature organization, so activities are well documented and easy to share with new employees and prospective clients to get approval. For CSI, procedures are not documented, but tactics and techniques are. Through the training and testing regimen of new employees, they're allowed to determine their own procedures and have to be able to explain them to their peers. This is done to ensure the employee can explain them to future clients as well.

During the early planning phase, these processes and procedures were presented to stakeholders in documents explaining what the engagement would entail. Each section had a header that covered the tactics they would be using and what it would target on a possible threat actor's side. Stakeholders were allowed to ask questions and decide which tactics would be used within the environment. Some procedures were denied due to the impact they could have on operations.

At the same time, the team was doing additional research on the client's network and identified some activities they believed would be good to get approved ahead of time. One of these was immediate network disconnection for a confirmed malicious C2 implant on a non-critical endpoint. These activities were presented to the stakeholders before all agreements were finished to get approval. Some activities were approved, and others were decided to be on an *as-requested* basis with authority resting in, and permission given by, the **chief operating officer (COO)** once the agreement was signed.

The COO has most of the authority that pertains to the team throughout the engagement. The only authority they don't have pertains to some small—but extremely sensitive— research and development network. The authority for taking action on that network resides with the CEO. For pre-approved actions that need permission, the COO will be involved in all discussions, with the CEO only involved in the small **research and development (R&D)** network.

The agreement is titled *CSI Engagement Contract* but represents the same documentation as an **MOU**. It lists time, resources, approved activities, and deliverables at the end and has legally binding clauses that are reviewed by both the client's and CSI's lawyers. Once they are signed by the CEO and the CSI sales lead, the hunt team can really get started with in-depth planning and communication.

All these activities—the start of planning, MOU agreement, activity research, procedure discussion—take place at the same time at the start of the engagement. This is not a step-by-step process but many steps taking place at the same time with various members of the client organization to ensure the right people are looking at the right documentation; for example, the COO isn't going to know which procedures and processes will impact the network at the detail needed by the hunt team to fully understand the impacts of their actions. Those documents go to the technical lead for that team to review and advise the COO. Meanwhile, the COO will be working through the documentation, deliverable, and communication requirements with the other stakeholders. The start of a hunt is a very dynamic and chaotic time, which is why the *CSI* team has focused so hard on communication and documenting the processes to get approval.

Summary

We covered how critical communication is at each step of a hunt in the earlier chapters. If anything needs to persist, ensure that it is documented in a complete and verbose enough manner that the reader will understand the intent. There are three main approaches to TTP documentation—balance these approaches with the capability and maturity of the hunt team and the acceptable risk level of the target organization.

Each threat hunt will require its own agreement between the team and the customer. That agreement will need to be signed by the individual or individuals with the appropriate authority to grant permission for the requested activities. Do not hesitate to involve lawyers in this phase. Pre-approved actions should be outlined in the agreement. Do not skip this!

In the next chapter, we will begin discussing activities that happen during and after a hunt, along with deliverables. This is where the documentation discussed in this chapter comes into play, as poor documentation often leads to poor deliverables and low client satisfaction.

Review questions

Answer the following questions to check your knowledge of this chapter:

1. Processes and procedures can be broken down into which three categories?
2. (True or false) An MOA is a signed and approved plan that specifies all of the requirements and expectations of a hunt.
3. (True or false) Lawyers never need to be involved in confirming or receiving authorities for a hunt team.

4. Which is not an example of something that is normally listed in the authorization?

    A.   Time period authorization is valid for

    B.   Data the team is authorized to interact with

    C.   The travel methods the team must use

    D.   Explicit unauthorized actions

5. _____ are actions that increase the overall risk and require notification to team leaders that they were taken or are about to be executed.

6. _____ are actions that drastically increase the overall risk and require permission from the customer before executing them.

Review answers

The answers to the review questions are as follows:

1. TTPs

2. True

3. False

4. C

5. Pre-approved actions

6. Non-approved actions

Part 3: Recovery – Post-Hunt Activity

Here, you will gain an understanding of the actions required of a team once a hunt is completed.

This part of the book comprises the following chapters:

12
Deliverables

What is the difference between a group of individuals that *do things* and a focused team accomplishing tasks? If we put aside the colorful words, it's the deliverables that make a difference. A lot of time and effort goes into threat hunting, but if everyone simply moves on with their lives once it is done, then most of that effort will be wasted and pointless before they even leave the facility.

Throughout the entire threat hunting process, communication and detailed documentation will have occurred in each phase. The final deliverables are where all of this *extra* effort shows its worth and why certain threat hunting teams are requested time and time again, while others are quickly forgotten. The first few times a team produces deliverables in the form of documentation, the process will be stressful. The team may not have prepared ahead of time, members may have slacked on their documentation throughout the hunt, data may have been missed or even deleted, and everyone is tired and ready for a break.

The trick is to do most of the work before the hunt even begins. Build up a stockpile of various templates that can be used. Having these templates ready to go will allow leads to update them with some minor notes and screenshots at the end of each shift. When the time comes to finalize deliverables, all that needs to be done is to pare down the data into reports and summarize and re-word the information so that it is appropriate for the intended audience. Under a time crunch, it is much easier to rework a product than to generate a new one from scratch.

In this chapter, we are going to cover the following topics:

- What to say and what not to say
- Confidence levels
- Knowing your audience
- Products for local defenders
- Types of reports
- Reporting timelines
- Scenario A—internal threat hunt
- Scenario B—external threat hunt

By the end of the chapter, you will be able to do the following:

- *Identify* the standard timelines of various deliverables that are produced during a threat hunt.
- *Comprehend* the different target audiences, along with what information should be conveyed to them.
- *Discuss* the various types of reports that are beneficial for a customer.

What to say and what not to say

Before we get into the various types of products and deliverables, we need to discuss the elephant in the room (again) – communication.

The words, pictures, and graphs that the team decides to use have meaning and power beyond what the team intends them to convey. These images and words will be received by an audience that you do not directly interface with and the team will not have the ability to adjust that perception after the fact. The audience you write the report for isn't the only audience that interprets it. The report could be utilized in legal proceedings or leaked to the press. What you produce will be out in a world that is beyond your control.

> **Real-World Example**
>
> After a lengthy threat hunt, the team included a briefing for the executive leadership in their deliverables on everything that was identified and the perceived root causes of any adversarial activity. During this hunt, an intrusion began as a user was compromised by a web redirect on a website that they visited. The briefing explained what could have prevented such an attack and any recommended remediations, all centered on network improvements.
>
> During this portion of the brief, one of the senior executives asked who the individual was. As it was their network, a name was provided, after which that executive wrote down their information. The team did not find out whether anything went back to the individual on what transpired or whether any adverse reaction occurred.

Here, the team can include pictures in reports and briefings. Being told that an intrusion happened can be interpreted in a variety of ways based on the individual and their experiences. There are fewer ways to interpret a picture of highlighted logs showing the intrusion occurring. Use this superpower with care. Use it too much and a report can come across as lacking detail, while if you don't use it enough, people could miss the important piece you need them to focus on. And as always, know your audience. If you intend to show screenshots and captures of logs to a non-technical audience, keep the details at a high enough level that you do not lose their focus. Executives do not care about bugs, exploit chains, and auditing patterns; they care about time and money – the resources that are used to deal with the current threat and precious resources to fix the problem and the justification for it.

Confidence levels

Another way to help control and manage the message that the team presents to the client is by adopting an intelligence community's common vernacular. For years, that community has conveyed information in degrees of confidence based on the source, how trustworthy the source was, and the age of the information. With a little time investment, we can use the same template when presenting pieces of information. A detailed directive that's been published by the Office of the Director of National Intelligence can be found on their website at `https://www.dni.gov/files/documents/ICD/ICD%20 203%20Analytic%20Standards.pdf`:

- **Low level of confidence**: This is for data that has been fragmented, poorly corroborated, source data that can easily be modified/removed, or where large gaps in analysis or evidence exist.

- **Medium level of confidence**: This is for data that has been retrieved from a source that can be corroborated, or only has minor gaps in analysis and evidence.

- **High level of confidence**: This is for data where all the necessary sources provide corroborating information and each piece verifies the findings of the others.

Now, let's use the aforementioned confidence levels in a statement that would normally be conveyed to a customer. The first example is something that, while more natural sounding, should not be stated. The second example incorporates the appropriate talking points and sticks to the facts of what the hunt team can provide with minimal room for misinterpretation.

Do not state: "*We saw John's account downloading data from the file server and transmitting it to the threat actor's C2 server to sell it on the darknet.*"

Instead, say: "*With a high degree of confidence, our analysts have assessed that the account "John.Smith" was utilized by a threat actor to retrieve sensitive information from the enterprise and that it was exfiltrated from the network.*"

In this example, care needs to be taken to convey that it was an account taking the action, not the individual. Additionally, you must separate known facts from assumptions in the final deliverables. Unless the team can ascertain the purpose and origin of an external entity or what the adversary was trying to achieve, do not include it in the report. Remember, an audience for this report could end up in legal proceedings and you may have to defend the report.

The following is another example of two ways to say the same thing. The first method should not be used as it is not necessarily factual and leaves it up to each person receiving the information to interpret it. The second method is more in line with the standard use of confidence levels and only provides facts to the customer.

Do not state: "*The threat actor is not present on the network.*"

Instead, say: "*With a medium degree of confidence, our analysts have assessed that the hypothesis concerning the adversary being present on the network is false. This is based on the datasets being analyzed for the specified time frames that are available to the team.*"

In this example, the first line conveys that the adversary is not there and everything is fine. While this might be the findings of the team, it was based on a scoped assessment and numerous restrictions and limitations. Always be upfront about what was and was not accomplished, and the manner it occurred in.

Additionally, any final report or briefing should outline everything that aided or detracted from the specific rating, such as "*with the x, y, and z data sources missing we were unable to analyze this portion of the network and cannot assess that area at this time.*" Control the message and how the audience perceives it as much as possible.

Know your audience

When you're attempting to target a message concerning a threat hunt for an audience, there are two things to consider. The first is whether the audience is technical or whether they are concerned with technical actions. If the audience is the local defenders who protect the enterprise each day, then a technical brief and report would be the correct choice. They will be concerned with items such as specific log types, ports, and services that were exploited during an attack.

If the audience is executives that do not have a technical background, then that level of detail will cause issues. They may simply stop actively receiving information and space out as soon as something comes up that they cannot follow quickly. Another possible side effect is that the individual may spend more time during a briefing trying to understand a particular detail and miss other key points that the team wanted to convey.

Regardless of your audience, ensure that the team does not come across as the harbinger of doom and destruction. Do not be negative in tone or word choice. Presenting non-stop issues and concerns to an audience without any way out is a guaranteed way to become discredited, ignored, and not be asked back for additional hunts. The deliverables should strike a neutral tone throughout. While the information that is being conveyed might be correct, a path forward will need to be identifiable at the end of the discussion.

Finally, deliverables are not the place for salacious or other embarrassing information to be released. If, during the hunt, the team identifies workers who are misusing corporate workstations to play video games, look at adult material, or run side businesses, the final deliverables *are not* the time and place to share that information. The team lead will need to professionally communicate with the stakeholders on the evidence that's been discovered. Threat hunts are not about catching and embarrassing individuals – they're about proving the hypotheses and finding threat actors.

Products for local defenders

Except in extreme circumstances, most hunts will be executed with the aid of local defenders that staff the front lines of network defense every day. Providing these individuals with usable deliverables during and after the conclusion of the hunt is a major boon for the customer and reflects well on the hunt team. Some common products that can be provided are as follows:

- Network maps and an overview of how they were acquired
- Queries that were used during the hunt, along with descriptions of the associated indicators they would identify
- A technical report outlining all of the steps that were taken by the threat hunt team
- The intelligence report that the threat hunt was based on, as well as subsequent updates
- Detailed descriptions of evidence that was found that's related to threat actor activity
- Mappings of findings in evidence and intelligence to the MITRE ATT&CK framework
- A list of recommendations for improvements to increase the confidence level of the defenders' findings (or lack of)
- Common industry best practices and improvements for the network, defenders, and administrators

Even if these products are not requested, it is always a good idea to offer them to the individuals that would benefit from them. They will typically cost the hunt team nothing in terms of resources while providing *goodwill* and enhancing the interpersonal relationships with the local defenders. A little support like this can go a long way in boosting relationships, as well as growing the networks of competent peers.

Types of reports

Regardless of the size and scope of a hunt, a final report will always be generated for the client. This will fall into one of the following three categories:

- **Executive-level report**: This will be a high-level report for non-technical individuals or anyone that needs to understand the business-level impacts of what occurred. It will include the following:
  - An executive summary
  - Activities that were taken by the team

- The data that was analyzed
- A brief overview of the intelligence that was used
- High-level planning (the hypotheses to be answered, all assumptions and limitations, and more)
- The results of the hunt, along with the level of confidence for each hypothesis that was answered
- Any incidents that were uncovered during the hunt based on their severity level, observed dwell time, incident name, and description
- Things that would need to be modified/changed/added to improve the confidence level
- Recommendations to improve the environment, including listing the disciplines that will be required to implement them

- **Technical report**: This will be a detailed report for a technical audience and low-to mid-level management. It will include the following:

  - A high-level planning overview
  - A summary of the statistics of the hunt, the number of incidents, associated TTPs, and actionable recommendations for the technical audience
  - Detailed steps that were taken by the team, including any high-value commands and queries
  - Specific data points that were of benefit or lacked fidelity
  - The results of the hunt, along with the level of confidence for each hypothesis that was answered
  - Any incidents that were uncovered during the hunt based on their severity level, observed dwell time, incident name, and description
  - An overview of the observed adversarial TTPs and recommendations for detection mechanisms to find those actions
  - Things that would need to be modified/changed/added to improve the confidence level
  - Detailed recommendations with links to instructions, products, best practices, and more

- **Intelligence report**: This is an optional report based on the intelligence that has been gathered during the hunt. The need for this would be based on a request from the customer and/or findings that the threat hunt team thought were of strong value to the customer.

These are just three sample reports that can be provided and mixed, depending on the target audience. Always figure out what works best for your teams' stakeholders and mold the deliverable to meet their needs. Whatever the team produces, it must always be factual and to the point. Never embellish, overlook, or exclude anything that occurred, even if the customer asks you to.

Reporting timelines

Reporting can be done in a variety of ways and on a myriad of different timelines. These cycles will all depend on the requirements of the organization and the level of insight that they require. For example, it is not uncommon to submit an *end-of-day* summary to the stakeholders informing everyone of what was accomplished, any meaningful findings, and the milestones that are coming up for the team. Such communication can be submitted in an email or a summarized report. These tend to be short and to the point without any flair, such as graphics or charts. Unless something significant occurred, feedback will rarely be given for this type of deliverable.

If an extended threat hunt is being conducted, such as one that spans more than a month, it is not uncommon to have the hunt planned out in phases. After each major phase, a wrap-up report would be provided. This would be delivered in the same manner and formatting as an end-of-mission debrief with all the stakeholders. This type of report should include insights into all the significant events, the timeliness of completing all milestones, and graphics for anything of value that was identified.

Scenario A – internal threat hunt

The threat hunt progresses for the new team, as built by Widget Maker Inc. Hypotheses are tested, some are proved to be true, and others are discarded or modified based on new criteria. Eventually, the primary objectives of determining the applicability of the FBI's notification and improving the defenses for intellectual property are completed. Now, it is time to develop the final deliverables for the report to give to the interested parties.

Early on in the threat hunt, the stakeholders made it clear that they wanted both a leadership report and a technical report. Because of this, the team lead has been working with stakeholders on a template based on the end-of-day updates, so their familiarity with them will improve the team's understanding. The technical reports will follow the format of similar reports that have been utilized in the SOC.

The leadership report is written mostly by the team lead, with some assistance from the intelligence team member. The leadership report is broken up into sections that will flow naturally and are based on a few example *Executive Summary Report* templates found online.

It starts with a summary that consists of no more than six sentences that cover the entire engagement. After that, a breakdown of the individual hypotheses is provided; here, they specify why they were chosen and what actions were taken under each hypothesis. A high-level listing of the data that was analyzed and the confidence of each type of data and why it was relevant to the threat hunt is also provided.

Next, a list of the pertinent intelligence rated at a high confidence level is provided. The team lead knows that if a lower confidence level is used, the stakeholders will focus on it and the rest of the report will lose its impact. Also, the intelligence section must be carefully edited to ensure no information is shared about the tools, sources, or names that have been used that could compromise the intelligence professional's ability to find data in the future.

The next section contains the results regarding the outcome of each hypothesis listed. The team lead knows this double reinforcement will help the stakeholders focus on what they identified as priorities and how the team addressed them. This will help the team get additional resources in the future since it shows they're focused and aligned with organizational desires. Each of these results will have a confidence level associated with it and each listing with medium confidence or lower will explain exactly why it's at that level.

Finally, there's the recommendations section. The team lead has decided to break this into three different sections. The first must flow directly from the preceding section and provide recommendations to ensure the next hunt has the necessary high confidence findings. The next section must contain a list of recommendations to help enhance the protection of intellectual property. Finally, the last section is about improving the security of the environment that did not fit into the two prior sections. The team lead even includes a recommendation for additional employees – for example, a full-time CISO. The last part of the recommendations section groups each recommended action into a "*now, soon, later*" prioritization for the stakeholders to easily identify the most important aspects.

The technical report is reviewed by the team lead but is mostly written by the analysts. It follows the leadership report but does not have an executive summary. Instead, that section is broken out to detail the entire timeline of events in paragraphs. The team lead decides that this section should be limited to two pages to make sure the report isn't too long. Each hypothesis and action is broken down into more detailed tasks that include the procedural details of the actions aligned with each hypothesis. A technical listing of the data sources, including the operating system and firmware versions, is included.

The intelligence section is the same as what was prepared for the leadership report. That section has already been vetted as released and the technical report should not contain additional detail.

These recommendations are specific and provide links to vendors' best practices regarding their configuration and suggestions about new tools to implement to control any weaknesses. Further justification is provided for each recommendation; this includes the recommendations of personnel. The team lead did this because they know that the technical personnel will have to continue to advocate for these changes and having additional evidence based on a report is very powerful. The technical report also includes the "*now, soon, later*" prioritization list.

The team lead presents the report to the stakeholders at a specified time a few weeks after the declaration of the end of the hunt. There is a question-and-answer session after the report to allow the stakeholders to clarify any sections. Finally, the team lead does a hot wash with the threat hunt team to determine how to write the reports in the future. There is no presentation for the technical report, but the team lead does offer to answer questions via email later.

Scenario B – external threat hunt

CSI continues to hunt and prove the majority of their hypotheses. The ones that aren't proven are either modified so that they align with the new data the hunt has produced or are removed to determine how the incorrect and non-modifiable hypothesis was produced. As part of the initial agreement, and the standard for all CSI engagements, a threat intelligence brief, leadership, and technical report must be developed.

The threat intelligence brief is culled from all the intelligence that was produced during the threat hunt. It is carefully edited to remove any loss of intelligence gathering abilities for CSI in the future. The report is not a standard work document. Many graphics must go into the report to detail how this organization's threat profile from the darknet compares to organizations in the same business. Some of the findings point out that they're not doing as well as their peers in controlling data, credentials, and other areas of interest to threat actors.

These graphics are paired with an explanation of the findings that's no longer than two sentences. The recommendations that are provided at the end of the report are separated into a 3-, 6-, and 12-month prioritization. The recommendations are not highly technical because they address the intelligence weaknesses of the organization versus their technical issues. Many of the recommendations are process and procedure improvements.

The leadership brief is based on the template that CSI uses for all engagements. The first section contains the executive summary, which is ideally a quarter of a normal printed page but no longer than half a page. It covers the reason for the engagement of the threat hunting team, as well as their priorities, main hypothesis, results, and the confidence level of proving that hypothesis.

After the executive summary, a timeline of significant events is provided, including the events that caused the threat hunting team to be engaged. Then, the data sources are listed at a high level, and they are categorized into their respective confidence levels and the reasons for being assessed as either medium or low.

After that, high-level planning diagrams are shown, tying hypotheses to data and actions. Depending on the organization, the design and review of these diagrams can identify unintended isolation or over-connectedness. Alongside these diagrams, short two- or three-sentence descriptions of either a success or a challenge for each of the hypotheses are provided. The diagrams also show how the team addressed the priorities from the *Memorandum of Understanding* that was developed at the beginning of the engagement.

The results from the hunt are explained in further detail here, with clear descriptions and reasons why a piece of evidence was assessed at a certain confidence level. Color coding is used with the confidence levels and lows are listed first, ending with the high confidence data. CSI does this purposefully to ensure this section ends with a *good* or *upbeat* demeanor.

After establishing an upbeat demeanor, what follows the list of positives is a list of recommendations on how to improve those data sources. It is written very plainly so that it's easy to fit into an expenditure justification. Pictures are included if they're relevant to the recommendation. For example, if a piece of equipment has been severely damaged, a picture would be included to provide evidence of that.

Finally, the recommendation for the overall environment is included. This is also listed in a 3-, 6-, and 12-month schedule to provide some prioritization. The recommendations have links to best practices, products, or even personnel positions. For this report, the team lead has recommended a complete overhaul of the IT structure to build cybersecurity from the ground up. It also includes the previously mentioned recommendations for data confidence improvement so that the stakeholders can go straight to that section when planning for expenditures.

The technical report contains all the data from the first report. It will also contain any command output for interesting data that was found. If malicious code was identified, it will be mentioned in the hunt results section and further expanded on in an appendix. CSI and the technical teams appreciate seeing what leadership is receiving.

Once the reports are delivered, the team lead is asked to produce another report just for higher executives and board members. It is asked to be no longer than two pages long, but it must capture the actions, findings, and major recommendations. The team works to cut the report down to two full pages. The use of tables and diagrams is greatly increased in an attempt to still share the relevant data. The team lead later learns that that two-page document and the intel report were used by the CEO to brief the partners and investors on the need for rapid investment in maturing the cybersecurity posture of the network.

Summary

Throughout this chapter we covered several ways in which post-hunt activity is concluded and received by the stakeholders. Do the prep work for deliverables before the hunt begins. In turn, you will be able to update the deliverable templates throughout the hunt while the information is still fresh. Throughout this process, always be mindful of how and what is communicated as it can be interpreted or utilized beyond the team's control as soon as it is out of their hands.

Adopt the use of confidence levels (low, medium, and high) when discussing what has been observed. Know the audience that is being communicated with along with what their drivers and interests in the topic might be. There are three types of reports that are commonly produced, so target each one at its intended audience by using purposeful wording and select visual aids.

In the next and final chapter, we will review some key considerations for post-hunt activities. We will focus heavily on ways to mature a hunt team and quickly bring them from a loose group of people into a thriving, well-coordinated security defense team.

Review questions

Answer the following questions to test your knowledge of this chapter:

1. (True or False) It is best to always provide as many details as possible when you're briefing senior leaders within an organization.

2. A _____ level of confidence is used for data that has minor gaps in analysis.

3. A _____ level of confidence is used for data that is fragmented or poorly corroborated.

4. An executive-level report will typically contain which of the following?

   A. Activities that have been taken by the team

   B. Detailed steps that have been taken by the team to include commands

   C. High-level planning

   D. Specific data points that lacked fidelity

5. An _____ report can be optional and would need to be requested by the customer.

Review answers

The answers to the review questions are as follows::

1. False

2. Medium

3. High

4. A, C

5. Intelligence

13
Post-Hunt Activity and Maturing a Team

Once all the necessary work and effort has been put in place, the deliverables are sent to the stakeholders and the threat hunt is complete. Perhaps all the members have returned to their normal daily tempo or have moved on to the next threat hunt they've been contracted to execute. While this may feel like the time for the team to take a deep breath and relax, it is not yet time to lower the team's effort. The customer has received all the deliverables that they required, but it is now time for the threat hunt team to benefit from all the effort that has been put toward performing the hunt.

During this final phase of the team's hunting cycle, all members, including leadership, will need to have candid discussions concerning what did and did not occur and how it did or did not happen. Since everyone is going through this process, you must keep a few things in mind:

- Failure is an exceptionally common occurrence.
- Failure can be beneficial in the long run, so long as that failure is not repeated in the same way.

- If a negative event occurred, the entire team must know about it – even new members of the team who were not there for the event must know about it. Chances are that some of the team members' families will know what occurred and who messed up. Not talking openly about the event will only erode the trust each team member has for the other.

In this chapter, we are going to cover the following topics:

- Setting the stage for feedback
- Feedback rules of engagement
- Timeline reconstruction and where to concentrate
- Feedback on the good and the bad
- Fixing and updating documentation
- Scenario A – internal threat hunt
- Scenario B – external threat hunt

By the end of the chapter, you will be able to do the following:

- *Comprehend* the importance of receiving and documenting honest feedback.
- *Discuss* how to set up and facilitate a debriefing session.
- *Comprehend* how to continue to grow a team once a hunt has concluded.

Setting the stage for feedback

As we mentioned in *Chapter 5, Methodologies*, there should be a final debrief or feedback session. When that feedback must be received, just like all the prior debriefs, preparation is key, and the following team requirements contribute greatly to the team's progress:

- All members should arrive armed and ready to go with all of the notes that they accumulated throughout the event. Members should be encouraged to think about the main topics and write down their impressions, ideas, and more for discussion.

- Each member will need to come prepared to invest time in the discussion. If done correctly, these sessions can be completed in only an hour or two if the hunt was relatively short and uneventful. If the hunt lasted months, then set aside a few days of the team's time to walk through everything.

- Choose a member as a timekeeper. They will help keep the team on topic and on time for breaks.

- Choose a member as a note keeper. They will need to take notes actively throughout the discussion so that all the members can see them. Additionally, they will be responsible for transcribing those items for retrieval later.

- Isolate the team to remove any distractions and side conversations by non-team members that may take away from the feedback. It is fine for observers to be present but they will need to understand their role – to be quiet.

- Only an active member of the team can have a speaking role – *all* observers should only observe. It does not matter if the CIO of the hunt organization comes in and has an idea; if they did not take part in the hunt, then this is not the time for them to speak. This is a very personal event for all active members of the team where they have a chance to grow together. Outside influence can stifle this and prevent the team from reaching their true potential.

- Food and drink are awesome. Ensure that the team is comfortable; removing simple distractions such as hunger and thirst can go a long way.

While this is not an all-encompassing list, it is a good start. Always tailor the setting to the team and the personalities within it. Plan ahead and know how to react when certain *hot-button* issues arise that had caused a disagreement during the hunt. If you have an individual or two that likes to talk and dominate the conversation, know how you would like to ensure those that do not talk as much can still provide feedback without being talked over.

Feedback rules of engagement

Regardless of how many times the team has conducted a group feedback session, it is imperative to always start by outlining the **rules of engagement** (**ROEs**). This review sets the tone for the entire conversation and focuses the team's energy on the direction intended by the team lead.

The following are some examples of ROEs:

- Leave your feelings at the door; do not take things personally.
- Each active member of the team has an equal voice.
- Treat each other with respect – don't talk over one another.
- Focus on the problem, not the individual.
- Look at one item at a time and stay on track.
- Speak openly and directly – do not talk around the issue or concern.

- Stick to the facts – for example, this action happened at this time; this event was caused by this individual.

- If it is an assumption or perception, it needs to be introduced as such.

- If you saw something happen, chances are other people did as well. If it was negative, the team needs to correct the issue.

- And once again, always leave your feelings at the door and don't take things personally.

Real-World Example

While training members for a hunt team, a particular individual was repeatedly making egregious errors in judgment. During one portion of their training, they openly violated a core tenet of the team and was prevented from participating in any future missions. The next day, the team lead gathered all active members of the team and discussed what had happened. It was no surprise that all the members already had a good understanding of what had occurred, even if they were across the room when it happened.

The team was then asked whether the individual in question should receive another chance. Everyone present quickly said yes without any hesitation. The lead asked the question again but added whether each member trusted the individual to be a member of the team. Did they feel they were trustworthy to do the right thing, even if no one else was present? If so, would they be willing to vouch for the member? The room went silent and after a minute, each member changed their answer to no.

The individual in question was a good person; however, they had several shortcomings as a hunter that threatened the effectiveness of the team and the stability of any customer's network. Simply put, that individual should not have been a threat hunter without maturing some of their decision-making abilities. Separate feelings and attachments from the individual and focus on facts. As they say, "*It's not personal, it's business.*"

Just like when you're setting the stage, the ROEs listed previously are not all-inclusive. Figure out what works best for the hunt team and ensure that everyone understands them. When someone inevitably starts to break one of the rules, gently nudge them back into line and continue. While these are rules that everyone needs to adhere to, very rarely should a lead ever react negatively or harshly during feedback. Doing so will normally shut down the debrief and cause everyone to stop engaging.

If someone does become unruly, take a break and talk to that person alone. If they refuse to adhere to the ROEs, they need to be removed from the debriefing and the team should continue without them. Their feedback will need to be gathered at a later time in a one-on-one setting. Individual feedback should be provided to that person on why the debrief is important and how they could have negatively impacted the team.

Real-World Example

The discussions after a threat hunt mission were one of my favorite times of the entire engagement. If I led the mission, I would ensure that when the time came to highlight what happened, I started by listing the items I knew about that I could have done better. For all those missions where I tore my actions apart, I never had an individual treat me any different afterward or communicate that their faith in me had wavered.

This approach tended to lead the team toward being more open about what had transpired and less hesitant about highlighting something a more senior member did. These actions were understood to be addressing an action that happened and were not directed at the individual. When everything was done, members had built trust in one another through open and honest feedback.

Once the ROEs have been understood by everyone, it's time to begin a deeper dive into each area of concern or focus. Before the team can focus on any one area or topic, it is always best to ensure everyone is tracking the same baseline of what happened. In the next section, we will cover the concept of timeline reconstruction, which is utilized to do just this.

Timeline reconstruction and where to concentrate

How the feedback session is performed will be unique to each lead and their style. A general-purpose method would be to walk through the timeline in hourly increments if the hunt was only a few days long or tracked in daily increments if the hunt spanned weeks. At every step, stop and ask for any major events, and write them down on the board for the team to see.

This is not the time for reasoning or excuses. Stick to the facts of what happened and nothing more. Use the daily reports and notes to ensure events and impacts aren't lost. Like any other human activity, a threat hunt will become mundane most of the time and activities will bleed into each other.

The team is free to ask for clarification, but that is not the time to *fix* any issues or concerns that came up. Once the team has gone through the entire timeline and is looking at an expansive list of items to discuss, then go through them one more time.

This second time the team reviews the feedback, they should dig in and understand the root cause of what occurred during the events. If it was bad, discuss how to make sure it never happens again. If it was good, figure out how to repeat those successes. If an individual or individuals simply made a bad decision, that is fine. Figure out why and how everyone else can learn from their mistakes. Perhaps some processes can be put into place to make sure it doesn't happen, or a technological solution can be implemented.

Sometimes, the debrief can't get through the entire listing for a single event if it was very complicated. It's alright to take a lot of time and set it aside for further discussion later and continue moving through the feedback timeline. This is usually the best way since the momentum of getting through the debrief will be lost otherwise.

With the timeline reconstructed and everyone following the agreed-upon history of what occurred, it's time for everyone to provide feedback on how it went. This next section can be very hard for some individuals to embrace as it includes identifying both the good and bad events that occurred, along with identifying why they happened.

Feedback on the good and the bad

As this book has stated repeatedly, communication is a great and necessary thing, but what should the team discuss? Simple – absolutely everything that the team feels matters. When we say *team*, we mean absolutely that – anyone that was involved has an equal footing in providing feedback and insight into what happened. A senior member that had been on the team for 5 years has the same voice that should be listened to as a new person who is just learning what a hunt entails. Everyone can talk and when they do, everyone should listen to what they have to say.

The following is a sample flow for feedback discussions:

- ROE
- Planning
- Team preparation
- Execution – timeline reconstruction with items of interest highlighted:
  - Technically identifying malicious or abnormal activity
  - Threat intelligence inclusion throughout the hunt

- Reviewing and processing any findings
- Communication
- Deliverables and client feedback
- Highlighted items of interest
- Follow-on actions

If the stage is set correctly, the lead should direct the conversation and let the team take over the momentum. Throughout this process, the lead will need to nudge the team as needed to stay on course and move forward. It will not be uncommon for a few members to dominate the conversation; this can easily be remedied by the lead asking one of the quieter members a direct and open-ended question on the topic. Whenever possible, encourage the team to police themselves and motivate other members who might be hesitant to speak up.

Fixing and updating documentation

So, the team had a strong feedback session and wrote down a bunch of inputs the team could or should have done differently – it's not good if nothing happens with those inputs! The most common long-term fix is to update the documentation and training process. This could be in the form of team policies, training material or classes, and TTPs.

All of these actions will need to be categorized into short- and long-term items. Additionally, these items will be further divided into what is within the team's scope and what is outside of their scope. Anything that is within the team's scope should be assigned a point of contact within the team to *own* the fix. They will be responsible for documenting the item, applying the fix action, and working with all applicable stakeholders to make sure it sticks.

The fix actions that are outside the scope of the team will need to be briefed to the team's external leadership for potential follow-on action. Regardless of whether the fix is internal or external, the team lead will need to continue leading the team well after the hunt is completed. They are responsible for following up with each individual to track progress and provide additional direction as necessary.

The two biggest issues that personnel tend to run into while implementing long-term fix actions are authority and focus. Make sure that people have the authority to implement these actions. If they do not intrinsically have the required authority or cannot be granted it by the team, they may not be the correct point of contact. Focus can be aided by the follow-on that the lead provides well after the hunt. Long-term fixes tend to follow a version of the *Pareto principle* – solutions are completed to 80% and then gradually forgotten as the last 20% is the hardest. The whole team needs to come together to accomplish that last 20% as that's where the most value for the team resides.

Scenario A – internal threat hunt

The first threat hunt is truly complete – all the deliverables have been handed in and the team is ready to take a good break and work on improving their specific areas for next time, based on what each member feels is important. But the team leader for Widget Maker Inc.'s newest security section realizes that the final debrief, or feedback, is required for the threat hunt to be a full success.

The team lead communicates with the team and lets them know they'll spend at least the next 2 days going through this feedback together. This includes the network administrator, who thought they got out of the requirement and would be going back to the IT section. The team lead asks for and gets a volunteer as a timekeeper and gets some ideas for lunch and snacks for the next 2 days.

The team will do the feedback in the same space they conducted the hunt in. This will allow them to continue to control access, as well as using the daily logs, personal notes, and whiteboards that are already there. The day before the final debrief is scheduled to start, the ROEs are sent out. The email includes some of the following bits from the upcoming ROEs and then some:

- *"It's not personal, it's business – feedback will be blunt and honest, but without malice or intent to injure another team member."*

- *"Talk about problems, not people – someone may have a personal failing; this is not the forum for confrontation."*

- *"We're only here for the facts – no assumptions should be made."*

- *"We're a team; we all have the same voice."*

The team starts the feedback session by going over the ground rules, getting their notes in order, and discussing the flow of the next 2 days via a short planning session. Once that is complete, the timeline reconstruction process starts, and the team members start highlighting areas of concern they had, as well as their successes!

The team goes over how they didn't like how some of the data flow started in the beginning, identifying how it impacted the ability of the analysts to process data. Another area of interest is the problem with assigning work and ensuring that data is shared well without some ad hoc solution; they broach the idea of using a case management solution moving forward.

Another area that is discussed is the great work of the network administrator and intelligence analyst. Of course, there are items of interest in each of the areas where those team members worked well. The intelligence process having to integrate with whatever case management solution is being utilized is also recorded as a follow-on action.

All the follow-on actions are kept on a separate whiteboard, with volunteers for each of the items, and a secondary identified. They're also prioritized to ensure time isn't wasted pursuing something that isn't of greater value to the team.

Of course, with the team being new and very immature, this identifies a strong need for documentation and developing TTPs that work with their environment. Documentation isn't identified as the highest-priority follow-on action, but it is up there.

The team lead takes all the feedback and documents it separately in a plan for the team to review. Once they've done that, the plan is presented to the stakeholders and used as justification for further resources and the continued existence of the team. This also ensures that the team lead has the authority to make and delegate some of the changes the team requests, ensuring they'll continue to improve and learn from their failures during hunts.

Scenario B – external threat hunt

The CSI team has finished wrapping up and moved out of the office space provided to them by the company. All the items they had borrowed are returned, and the team heads home. After 1 day of recovering from traveling, the team lead shares the ROEs they utilized and asks everyone to prepare for feedback. It will be a 3-day event with food and drinks provided, and a presentation will be provided to the **chief of operations** (**COO**) when the feedback session has been completed.

The CSI team knows that the feedback process is integral to their high performance and one of the reasons they keep getting business offers to do hunts on a network. They know that the feedback process focuses on making each of them better, in addition to bettering their team as a whole. When the CSI is receiving feedback, the intelligence analyst will not be present. The contractor that's been utilized for the team is not a full-time member and may not even be used in the next few threat hunts.

The ROEs that the team lead shares are a little different from the ones that have been seen online or used in other organizations. Since the team has been together for over a year, the normal rules are already well known; all the team members know rules such as *"Don't make it personal."* Instead, the team lead has tailored a unique set of rules for the team to address their specific needs. This includes the following items:

- *"You can't be happy with everything – find something to improve."*

- *"Each member must provide at least one "devil's point of view" for each item of interest."*

- *"Team members can only be primary on two action items, and secondary on two action items."*

- *"It's alright to point out that you're annoyed at something small."*

The team will use both a physical and virtual space. They've got some of their tools to assist in the feedback session. The first half of the feedback session involves getting the presentation templates dusted off, reviewing their processes, and using the tools for each individual to build a personal timeline that will be combined with other team members into a single grand timeline to discuss.

As the team starts going through the combined timeline, each area of interest is discussed, led by the individual who marked it on their timeline. The team members can either voice their concerns out to the group, add to an anonymous question or feedback area, or provide amplifying information directly to the timeline during this process.

One area of action moving forward is the lack of flexibility in the deliverables the team is required to deliver. When some interesting findings occur that are outside the deliverable template's structure, it is difficult to write the final report so that it flows because of what's dictated by the template. Another item involves some of the challenges that were faced by the contract intelligence professional. The intelligence analyst worked out fine, but the lack of synergy at the beginning was time-consuming to overcome and their deliverable had to be worked on a lot because it didn't match the style of CSI's other reports.

At the end of the timeline review and action item stage, the team lead reminds everyone about the restrictions, as per the ROEs, on the number of action items they could work on. There is some lobbying on who would work on what item, but a happy resolution is achieved when some light bribing is done. Everyone knows they'll have to work on updating documentation for their area and have to review the updated documentation for each other's areas.

After that, they work on the presentation for the COO, one of the four founding CSI members, to identify areas for improvement and investment. The team lead presents it a week later without any issue. The COO asks whether there are any areas the team lead feels they lacked authority or needed support to make continued changes. The team lead says there aren't any at the moment, but it is always something the team is watchful for. After a reasonable amount of time is spent trying to improve themselves and the team based on the action items, the team is ready for another threat hunt.

Summary

Failure is common and should be expected – strive to not fail the same way twice. Feedback after the hunt is critical in allowing the team to grow and in their level of effectiveness. Direct and open feedback is needed to allow this to happen. Once items have been identified for improvement with applicable actions, the lead will need to follow up to ensure that they take root.

Some of the items in this book might be concepts that are contrary to how your current team or organization operates. The simple act of identifying what went wrong and then spending resources to fix it might be contrary to your current leadership methodology. Does this mean that the current team is ineffective and needs to be rebuilt from the ground up? No.

This entire book centered around a few key concepts and then expounded upon them in various ways. Identify what can positively fit in your current structure and then grow it from there. Remember that communication is central to everything a team does – only through purposeful and effective communication will a team grow. In turn, the message that is sent through that communication will drive the culture that the members experience.

An organization's culture is felt through all the verbal and nonverbal communication that the organization conveys every day. Changing this underlying culture of an organization is not something that can be done by writing a memo or creating a new policy. It is something that requires constant pressure and positively applying reinforcement from leadership.

While this may conclude a phase of the development and maturing of a hunt team, it does not have to end here. Continue to press your advantage and evolve each aspect of your team in order to strive for a more efficient and effective version of what you were. Seek out peers in the same field to learn from one another, find those that are successful, and emulate what makes them great. Share your story and journey with others so that they can follow in your steps.

Review questions

Answer the following questions to test your knowledge of this chapter:

1. When you're setting the stage for feedback, which of the following is not a role that someone should be assigned?

    A. Timekeeper

    B. Note keeper

    C. Facilitator

    D. Food manager

2. (True or False) When you're setting the stage for feedback, the location does not matter.

3. (True or False) If someone dominates the discussion during a debrief, it is alright to let them talk over everyone else.

4. (True or False) If there is a controversial event that occurred, it should not be covered in the team debrief.

5. What are the two biggest issues that teams tend to have for fix actions identified during a debrief?

Review answers

The following are the answers to this chapter's questions:

1. D

2. False

3. False

4. False

5. Lack of authority to implement the fix action; lack of focus for personnel to work on the fix action

Appendix

Acronyms

C2 – Command and control

CEO – Chief executive officer

CMF – Cyber management framework

COO – Chief operating officer

CSF – Cybersecurity framework

CSI – Cybersecurity intelligence

DMZ – Demilitarized zone

DOS – Denial of service

EDR – Endpoint detection and response

EPS – Events per second

FBI – Federal Bureau of Investigation

IDS – Intrusion detection system

IOC – Indicator of compromise

IPS – Intrusion prevention system

IT – Information technology

MOA – Memorandum of agreement

MOE – Measurement of effectiveness

MOP – Measurement of performance

MOU – Memorandum of understanding

MS-ISAC – Multi-State Information Sharing and Analysis Center

NOC – Network operations center

NIST – National Institute of Standards and Technology

OSINT – Open source intelligence

OT – Operational technology

PaaS – Platform as a service

PCAP – Packet capture

PCI – Payment Card Industry

PCI DSS – Payment Card Industry Data Security Standard

POV – Point of view

ROE – Rule of engagement

RFI – Request for information

RFID – Radio-frequency identification

SIEM – Security information and event management

SOC – Security operations center

SOW – Statement of work

TI – Threat intelligence

TTP – Tactic, technique, and procedure

Definitions

Assumption: An occurrence or finding that the team is planning on being either true or false.

Behavioral-based hunt: A hunt with a low intelligence level and a high network knowledge level.

Client system administrator: A role that is focused on the existing administrators of the target network.

(Low) Confidence: This is associated with data that is fragmented or poorly corroborated, source data that can easily be modified/removed, or where large gaps in analysis or evidence exist.

(High) Confidence: This is associated with data in which all the necessary sources provide corroborating information and each piece verifies the findings of the others.

(Medium) Confidence: This is associated with data that is retrieved from a source that can be corroborated, or only has minor gaps in analysis and evidence.

Constraint: A limitation or restriction that's placed by an outside force or entity. This includes those by higher-level organizations and legal or regulatory authorities.

Debrief: The briefing that's conducted at the end of a shift or threat hunt.

Direct analysis: A direct, or first-hand, observation of an event.

Execution: The phase during a threat hunt in which all the actions by the threat hunters take place.

Executive report: A high-level report for non-technical individuals or anyone that needs to understand the business-level impacts of what occurred.

False negative: The lack of a trigger by reactive defenses on abnormal or malicious system behavior or communications during analysis; for example, an adversary emulating an administrator to successfully exfiltrate data from the network.

False positive: An alert that is triggered by reactive defenses that is invalid, meaning that it does not meet the intent of the signature or heuristics that it was triggered by; for example, an intrusion prevention system firing on someone searching the internet for `testmyids.com`.

Host-based analyst: A role in a threat hunting team where the position requires high technical knowledge and focuses on all things that occur on workstations and servers.

Hybrid data collection: A data collection mindset of collecting as much data as possible and quickly scoping it down to only meaningful datasets.

In-band communication: A process where the target network is utilized to transfer data to or from the hunt team.

Incident responder: A role within an organization that focuses on investigating perceived malicious activity to identify the root cause and scope of the event.

Indicator of compromise: A piece of data, commonly found in logs, that shows potential malicious activity on an enterprise or system.

Input-driven data collection: A data collection mindset of collecting everything possible.

Intel-based hunt: A hunt with a high intelligence level and a low network knowledge level.

Intelligence report: An optional report based on the intelligence that's been gathered during the hunt.

IOC/anomaly-based hunt: A hunt with a high intelligence level and a high network knowledge level.

Intelligence: The level of understanding about the adversary the organization is concerned about.

Measurement of effectiveness: The documented intended effect based on completing one or more measurements of performance(s).

Measurement of performance: The documented tactical action required to achieve a specific outcome.

Methodologies: The framework and structure that the details for a threat hunt are built on to keep processes aligned and provide all stakeholders with a repeatable process.

Network administrator: A role in a threat hunting team that is responsible for ensuring all the infrastructure and equipment that's utilized by the hunt team is in working order throughout the mission.

Network-based analyst: A role in a threat hunting team that requires high technical knowledge and focuses on all things that occur across the network.

Network knowledge: The amount of detailed understanding of the target network.

Operational threat intelligence: A highly detailed version of intelligence that contains detailed information on things such as forensically analyzing toolsets and an adversary's known tactics, techniques, and procedures.

Out-of-band communication: The process where a separate network other than the target network is utilized to transfer data to or from the hunt team.

Output-driven data collection: A data collection mindset that focuses on collecting only what the team believes that they need.

Prebrief: The briefing that is conducted before the start of any shift or work.

Procedure: Very specific directions and requirements an individual should follow to achieve the desired outcome.

Radical transparency: The concept of promoting complete openness within an organization.

Random hunt: A hunt with a low intelligence level and a low network knowledge level.

Restraint: A limitation or restriction that's put in place by an internal force or entity. This includes restraints from internal organizational stakeholders and the policy or the hunt team.

Scope: A documented list of the target systems, networks, and intentions of the team as it pertains to that particular threat hunt.

Secondary correlation: An indirect, or second-hand, inference of an event based on the correlation of information from other sources.

Strategic threat intelligence: A high-level concept of intelligence that covers an actor's motivations and intentions and, potentially, their capabilities.

Tactic: A general, high-level concept or way of approaching a problem.

Team lead: A role in the threat hunting team whose purpose is to lead the team both from an internal as well as an external standpoint.

Technical report: A detailed report for a technical audience and low- to mid-level management.

Technique: Narrower in focus than a tactic, this includes specific mechanisms and high-level incorporation of the toolsets that *must* be utilized to accomplish the required action. For example, mentioning the need to retrieve the antivirus logs from each system would be incorporated into a technique. The toolset that's utilized to retrieve those logs would be part of the procedure.

Threat intel analyst: A role in a threat hunting team that specializes in acquiring, aggregating, and correlating threat intelligence related to the active threat hunt.

Trigger: An event- or time-based occurrence that will signify an action or actions to be performed.

True negative: The lack of a trigger by reactive defenses during the analysis of normal system behavior or communications.

True positive: An alert that is triggered by reactive defenses that is valid, in that it meets the intent of the signature or heuristics that triggered it; for example, an antivirus signature alerting of a Trojan that was downloaded.

Index

Packt.com

Subscribe to our online digital library for full access to over 7,000 books and videos, as well as industry leading tools to help you plan your personal development and advance your career. For more information, please visit our website.

Why subscribe?

- Spend less time learning and more time coding with practical eBooks and Videos from over 4,000 industry professionals
- Improve your learning with Skill Plans built especially for you
- Get a free eBook or video every month
- Fully searchable for easy access to vital information
- Copy and paste, print, and bookmark content

Did you know that Packt offers eBook versions of every book published, with PDF and ePub files available? You can upgrade to the eBook version at packt.com and as a print book customer, you are entitled to a discount on the eBook copy. Get in touch with us at customercare@packtpub.com for more details.

At www.packt.com, you can also read a collection of free technical articles, sign up for a range of free newsletters, and receive exclusive discounts and offers on Packt books and eBooks.

Other Books You May Enjoy

If you enjoyed this book, you may be interested in these other books by Packt:

Practical Threat Intelligence and Data-Driven Threat Hunting

Valentina Costa-Gazcón

ISBN: 9781838556372

- Understand what CTI is, its key concepts, and how it is useful for preventing threats and protecting your organization
- Explore the different stages of the TH process
- Model the data collected and understand how to document the findings
- Simulate threat actor activity in a lab environment
- Use the information collected to detect breaches and validate the results of your queries
- Use documentation and strategies to communicate processes to senior management and the wider business

Mastering Cyber Intelligence

Jean Nestor M. Dahj

ISBN: 9781800209404

- Understand the CTI lifecycle which makes the foundation of the study
- Form a CTI team and position it in the security stack
- Explore CTI frameworks, platforms, and their use in the program
- Integrate CTI in small, medium, and large enterprises
- Discover intelligence data sources and feeds
- Perform threat modelling and adversary and threat analysis
- Find out what Indicators of Compromise (IoCs) are and apply the pyramid of pain in threat detection
- Get to grips with writing intelligence reports and sharing intelligence

Packt is searching for authors like you

If you're interested in becoming an author for Packt, please visit `authors.packtpub.com` and apply today. We have worked with thousands of developers and tech professionals, just like you, to help them share their insight with the global tech community. You can make a general application, apply for a specific hot topic that we are recruiting an author for, or submit your own idea.

Share Your Thoughts

Now you've finished *The Foundations of Threat Hunting*, we'd love to hear your thoughts! Scan the QR code below to go straight to the Amazon review page for this book and share your feedback or leave a review on the site that you purchased it from.

`https://packt.link/r/180324299-X`

Your review is important to us and the tech community and will help us make sure we're delivering excellent quality content.

Made in the USA
Middletown, DE
24 April 2023

29417515R00137